HAMLET

POEM UNLIMITED

HAMLET

POEM UNLIMITED

HAROLD BLOOM

RIVERHEAD BOOKS

a member of Penguin Putnam Inc.

New York

2003

Riverhead Books
a member of
Penguin Putnam Inc.
375 Hudson Street
New York, NY 10014

Library of Congress Cataloging-in-Publication Data

Bloom, Harold.
Hamlet : poem unlimited / Harold Bloom.
p. cm.
ISBN 1-57322-233-X
1. Shakespeare, William, 1564–1616. Hamlet.
2. Hamlet (Legendary character). 3. Tragedy. I. Title.
PR2807.B617   2003   2002031691
822.3'3—dc21

Printed in the United States of America
1   3   5   7   9   10   8   6   4   2

This book is printed on acid-free paper. ∞

Book design by Stephanie Huntwork

For Nancy Dale Becker

and Robert A. Becker

I would like to acknowledge my two research assistants,

Aislinn Goodman and Yoojin Grace Kim,

and my editor, Celina Spiegel.

In the main I have followed the latest Arden edition,

but have repunctuated frequently, according

to my understanding of the text.

The best actors in the world, either for tragedy, comedy, history, pastoral, pastoral-comical, historical-pastoral, tragical-historical, tragical-comical-historical-pastoral, scene individable, or poem unlimited.

—Polonius

CONTENTS

HAMLET
POEM UNLIMITED

This short book is a postlude to my *Shakespeare: The Invention of the Human* (1998). In composing that full-scale work on all of Shakespeare's plays, I found myself obsessed with the relationship of *Hamlet* to an earlier, missing play, the so-called *Ur-Hamlet*. Most scholars, on inadequate grounds, ascribe that lost drama to Thomas Kyd, author of *The Spanish Tragedy*. I continue to follow the late Peter Alexander in believing that Shakespeare wrote both *Hamlet*s, so that he is revising himself in the great play of 1600.

Unfortunately, I became so concerned with matters

of origin that I devoted far too much of a long chapter to them, and ruefully realized only later that most of what I thought and felt about *Hamlet* remained unsaid. *Hamlet: Poem Unlimited* is the fulfillment of my desire to remedy my prior obsessiveness, and is offered now as a companion to *Shakespeare: The Invention of the Human*.

It is my hope, though, that I offer here something more than a supplement to the earlier, far larger volume. Shakespeare is my model and my mortal god, and *Hamlet: Poem Unlimited* therefore has a revisionary relationship to *Shakespeare: The Invention of the Human*. The enigma in confronting Shakespeare's plays is the question of Shakespeare himself. Where does he stand, implicitly, in relation to his own work? Four centuries have led most readers and playgoers to the strong conviction that Shakespeare's investment in *Hamlet* is more personal and more potentially illuminating than is his attachment to any of his other plays, including even *The Tempest*. Much of *Hamlet: Poem Unlimited* devotes itself to meditative surmises upon Shakespeare's involvement in the mysteries of his final *Hamlet*.

INFERRING HAMLET

amlet is part of Shakespeare's revenge upon revenge tragedy, and is of no genre. Of all poems, it is the most unlimited. As a meditation upon human fragility in confrontation with death, it competes only with the world's scriptures.

Contrary, doubtless, to Shakespeare's intention, *Hamlet* has become the center of a secular scripture. It is scarcely conceivable that Shakespeare could have anticipated how universal the play has proved to be. Ringed round it are summits of Western literature: the *Iliad*, the *Aeneid*, *The Divine Comedy*, *The Canterbury Tales*,

King Lear, Macbeth, Don Quixote, Paradise Lost, War and Peace, The Brothers Karamazov, Leaves of Grass, Moby-Dick, In Search of Lost Time, among others. Except for Shakespeare's, no dramas are included. Aeschylus and Sophocles, Calderón and Racine are not secular, while I suggest the paradox that Dante, Milton, and Dostoevsky are secular, despite their professions of piety.

HAMLET'S OBSESSIONS are not necessarily Shakespeare's, though playwright and prince share an intense theatricality and a distrust of motives. Shakespeare is in the play not as Hamlet, but as the Ghost and as the First Player (Player King), roles he evidently acted. Of the Ghost, we are certain from the start that he indeed is King Hamlet's spirit, escaped from the afterlife to enlist his son to revenge:

If thou didst ever thy dear father love—
[I.v.23]

The spirit does not speak of any love *for* his son, who would appear to have been rather a neglected child. When not bashing enemies, the late warrior-king kept

4

his hands upon Queen Gertrude, a sexual magnet. The graveyard scene (V.i) allows us to infer that the prince found father and mother in Yorick, the royal jester:

He hath bore me on his back a thousand times, and now—how abhorred in my imagination it is—my gorge rises at it. Here hung those lips that I have kissed I know not how oft.

[V.i.185–89]

Hamlet is his own Falstaff (as Harold Goddard remarked) because Yorick, "a fellow of infinite jest, of most excellent fancy," raised him until the prince was seven. The Grave-digger, the only personage in the play witty enough to hold his own with Hamlet, tells us that Yorick's skull has been in the earth twenty-three years, and that it is thirty years since Hamlet's birth. Yet who would take the prince of the first four acts, a student at the University of Wittenberg (a German Protestant institution, famous for Martin Luther), as having reached thirty? Like his college chums, the unfortunate Rosencrantz and Guildenstern, Hamlet can be no older than about twenty at the start, and the lapsed time represented in the tragedy cannot be more than eight weeks, at the most. Shakespeare, wonderfully careless on matters of time and space, wanted a preternaturally matured Hamlet for Act V.

Though we speak of act and scene divisions, and later in this little book I will center upon the final act, these are not Shakespeare's divisions, since all his plays were performed straight through, without intermissions, at the Globe Theatre. The uncut *Hamlet*, in our modern editions, which brings together all verified texts, runs to nearly four thousand lines, twice the length of *Macbeth*. *Hamlet* is Shakespeare's longest play, and the prince's role (at about fifteen hundred lines) is similarly unique. Only if you run the two parts of *Henry IV* together (as we should) can you find a Shakespearean equivalent, with Falstaff's role as massive, though unlike Hamlet my sublime prototype speaks prose only—the best prose in the language, except perhaps for Hamlet's.

The Tragical Historie of Hamlet, Prince of Denmarke stands apart among Shakespeare's thirty-eight plays, quite aside from its universal fame. Its length and variety are matched by its experimentalism. After four centuries, *Hamlet* remains our world's most advanced drama, imitated but scarcely transcended by Ibsen, Chekhov,

Pirandello, and Beckett. You cannot get beyond *Hamlet*, which establishes the limits of theatricality, just as Hamlet himself is a frontier of consciousness yet to be passed. I think it wise to confront both the play and the prince with awe and wonder, because they know more than we do. I have been willing to call such a stance Bardolatry, which seems to me only another name for authentic response to Shakespeare.

HOW SHOULD we begin reading *Hamlet*, or how attend it in performance, in the unlikely event of finding the play responsibly directed? I suggest that we try to infer just how the young man attired in black became so formidably unique an individual. Claudius addresses the prince as "my son," meaning he has adopted his nephew as royal heir, but also gallingly reminding Hamlet that he is a stepson by marriage. The first line spoken by Hamlet is, "A little more than kin, and less than kind," while the next concludes punningly, "I am too much in the sun." Is there an anxiety that Hamlet actually may be Claudius's son, since he cannot know for certain exactly when what he regards as adultery and incest began between Claudius and Gertrude? His notorious hesitations at hacking down Claudius stem partly from the sheer magnitude of his consciousness, but they may also indicate a realistic doubt as to his paternity.

We are left alone with Hamlet for the first of his seven soliloquies. Its opening lines carry us a long way into the labyrinths of his spirit:

O that this too too sullied flesh would melt,
Thaw and resolve itself into a dew . . .
                                    [I.ii.129–30]

The First Folio gives us "solid flesh," while the Second Quarto reads "sallied flesh." While "sallied" could mean "assailed," it is probably a variant for "sullied." Hamlet's recoil from sullied flesh justifies D. H. Lawrence's dark observation that "a sense of corruption in the flesh makes Hamlet frenzied, for he will never admit that it is his own flesh." Lawrence's aversion remains very striking: "A creeping, unclean thing he seems. . . . His nasty poking and sniffling at his mother, his traps for the King, his conceited perversion with Ophelia make him always intolerable." Though Lawrence's perspective is disputable, we need not contest it, because Lawrence himself did: "For the soliloquies of Hamlet are as deep as the soul of man can go . . . and as sincere as the Holy Spirit itself in their essence." We can sympathize with Lawrence's ambivalence: that "a creeping, unclean thing" should also be "as sincere as the Holy Spirit" is the essence of Hamlet's view of humankind, and of himself in particular.

The central question then becomes: How did Hamlet develop into so extraordinarily ambivalent a consciousness? I think we may discount any notion that the double shock of his father's sudden death and his mother's remarriage has brought about a radical change in him. Hamlet always has had nothing in common with his father, his mother, and his uncle. He is a kind of changeling, nurtured by Yorick, yet fathered by himself, an actor-playwright from the start, though it would not be helpful to identify him with his author. Shakespeare distances Hamlet from himself, partly by appearing on stage *at his side*, as paternal ghost and as Player King, but primarily by endowing the prince with an authorial consciousness of his own, as well as with an actor's proclivities. Hamlet, his own Falstaff, is also his own Shakescene, endlessly interested in theater. Indeed, his first speech that goes beyond a single line is also his first meditation upon acting:

> *These indeed seem,*
> *For they are actions that a man might play;*
> *But I have that within which passes show . . .*
>
> [I.ii.83–85]

In some sense, Hamlet's instructions to the actors go on throughout the play, which is probably the best of all textbooks on the purposes of playing. Hamlet is neither a philosopher nor a theologian, but an enthusiastic and remarkably informed amateur of the theater. He certainly seems to have spent more time playing truant at the Globe in London than studying at Wittenberg. The Ghost exits, murmuring, "Remember me," and we hear Hamlet reminding the Globe audience that he is one of them:

> *Remember thee?*
> *Ay, thou poor ghost, whiles memory holds a seat*
> *In this distracted globe.*
>
> [I.v.95–97]

Shakespeare might have subtitled *Hamlet* either *The Rehearsal* or *Unpack My Heart with Words*, for it is a play about playing, about acting out rather than revenging. *We* are self-conscious, but Hamlet is consciousness of *something*. For Hamlet, the play's the thing, and not just to mousetrap Claudius. At the very close, Hamlet fears a wounded name. I suggest that his anxiety pertains not to being a belated avenger, but to his obsessions as a dramatist.

TWO

HORATIO

With Horatio and Marcellus as his initial audience, Hamlet starts playing the antic, and will not cease until he abandons the graveyard scene, to act instead the apotheosis of his dying. Marcellus fades quickly away, but Horatio abides to tell Hamlet's story. William Hazlitt, a great critic, observed, "It is we who are Hamlet," but actually we are Horatio, Hamlet's perpetual audience, which is why Horatio is in the play. Though without visible means of support, and without either status or function at the Court of Elsinore, Horatio is omnipresent.

Horatio is a fellow student of Hamlet's at Wittenberg, and his age is even more ambiguous than Hamlet's, since he tells Marcellus in the play's first scene
that he saw King Hamlet battle against both Nor-
way and Poland, at the time of what turns out to have
been Prince Hamlet's birth. If Horatio is still at Wittenberg at forty-seven or so (at the least), he disturbs our
credulity, but Shakespeare doesn't care, and would have
been amused at our arithmetic. Hamlet, who shows little
enough evidence of affection for either Ophelia or Gertrude, manifests astonishing esteem for the startled
Horatio:

> *Since my dear soul was mistress of her choice,*
> *And could of men distinguish her election,*
> *Sh'ath seal'd thee for herself; for thou hast been*
> *As one, in suff'ring all, that suffers nothing,*
> *A man that Fortune's buffets and rewards*
> *Hast ta'en with equal thanks; and blest are those*
> *Whose blood and judgment are so well commeddled*
> *That they are not a pipe for Fortune's finger*
> *To sound what stop she please. Give me that man*
> *That is not passion's slave, and I will wear him*

In my heart's core, ay, in my heart of heart,
As I do thee.

[III.ii.64–74]

Only the audience, in suffering all, suffers nothing at a tragedy, and Horatio suffers so much when Hamlet is dying that he shocks us by attempting suicide. Hamlet's tribute is enigmatic, since the play permits Horatio only to be Hamlet's adoring straight man, and we simply are shown nothing of Horatio's supposed freedom from the slavery of passion. All that we know of Horatio is that Claudius does not even try to suborn him, which renders him unique at Elsinore. What matters is that Horatio loves Hamlet, and desires no existence apart from the prince. Though critics have asserted that Hamlet finds qualities in Horatio that are absent from himself, they plainly are mistaken. Hamlet is so various that he contains every quality, while Horatio, totally colorless, has none to speak of.

And yet there is no one else in all Shakespeare who resembles Horatio, whose gracious receptivity lingers on in our memories of the drama. Though many fight against idolatry of Hamlet, Shakespeare makes it difficult for us not to identify with Horatio, who is idolatrous. Horatio is Shakespeare's instrument for suborning the audience even as Claudius manipulates Elsinore: without Horatio, we are too distanced from the bewildering Hamlet for Shakespeare to work his guile upon us. Critics keep coming forward to protest that actually Hamlet is cold, brutal, a hero-villain at best. But such critics work against their own grain and ours, because they work against Shakespeare's subtle art. Horatio precisely is not Antony's freedman, Eros, who kills himself to "escape the sorrow / Of Antony's death." Eros is no more than a grace-note in *Antony and Cleopatra*; Horatio pragmatically is the most important figure in the tragedy except for Hamlet himself. Through Horatio we the audience contaminate the play.

That contamination is unique in Shakespeare, and is one of the elements that render *Hamlet* a class of one among Shakespeare's high tragedies. No other drama ever is so overtly audience-aware, or makes us so complicit in its procedures. In a curious sense, Shakespeare writes with Horatio and ourselves, rather as Iago composed with Othello, Desdemona, and Cassio, or Edmund with Edgar and Gloucester. Hamlet seems to write himself, and the other characters as well, except for Horatio.

Lest this seem my own madness, consider Horatio's one mild protest against Hamlet's imaginative extravagances in the graveyard:

> HAMLET *To what base uses we may return, Horatio!*
> *Why, may not imagination trace the noble dust of*
> *Alexander till a find it stopping a bung-hole?*
> HORATIO *'Twere to consider too curiously to consider so.*
>
> [V.i.202–206]

"Curiously" means something like "oddly," over-ingenious and on the wrong scale. Undeterred, Hamlet rushes on to clinch his point:

> *No, faith, not a jot, but to follow him thither with*
> *modesty enough, and likelihood to lead it. Alexander*
> *died, Alexander was buried, Alexander returneth to dust,*
> *the dust is earth, of earth we make loam, and why of*
> *that loam whereto he was converted might they not stop*
> *a beer-barrel?*
>
> [V.i.206–212]

Highest and lowest are one in the Hamlet-world. But they aren't for us, and our representative in that world is

Horatio. Where theatricalism governs all, and Hamlet is master of the revels, we hold fast to Horatio, who is too drab to be theatrical. We hope *we* are not drab, but we cannot keep up with Hamlet who is always out ahead of himself.

We may wonder, Where does Horatio find the eloquence that responds so beautifully to Hamlet's final "The rest is silence"? Horatio utters a hope—not a certainty—for an angelic chorus:

Now cracks a noble heart. Good night, sweet prince,
And flights of angels sing thee to thy rest.

[V.II.359–60]

We want Horatio's wish to be true, but Shakespeare's irony forestalls us. A drum sounds its beat, and a march of Norwegian soldiers replaces those wistful flights of angels.

THREE

PLAYS WITHIN PLAYS
WITHIN PLAYS

Hamlet probably was acted at the Globe during 1600, but it was for Shakespeare a highly volatile text, and in 1601 he seems to have expanded its ironic commentary on the War of the Theaters that he had with his rival/friend Ben Jonson. And yet even this Poets' War is only a portion of the maelstrom that constitutes the sequence that goes from Act II, Scene ii, line 315, through Act III, Scene ii, line 288. For almost a thousand lines, a fourth of the play, Shakespeare cuts a gap into his representation of reality, or imitation of an action. The Globe's audiences, on afternoons in 1601, evidently were sophisticated enough to accept an art that capriciously abandons the illusions of stage representation and then picks them up again.

Since I think that this freedom to forsake our legitimate expectations is central to *Hamlet* (and to Hamlet), I will elaborate upon Shakespeare's elliptical art, which I do not find illuminated by the term "metatheater." Hegel memorably said that Shakespeare's greatest characters were "free artists of themselves." Hamlet ought to be the freest, but Shakespeare prevents this, in order to maintain his own freedom to make at least this one play a "poem unlimited."

Why does Hamlet return to Elsinore after his sea adventure? Certainly it is not to complete his baffled revenge, now as defunct as the Ghost, or the son's memory of the father. Orson Welles had the happy fantasy that Hamlet goes to England, abandoning Denmark forever, and ages into Sir John Falstaff. This is akin to my own favorite fantasy, in which Falstaff declines to die of a broken heart, and finds himself again in the Forest of Arden, crunching Jaques and Touchstone in contests of wit and happily substituting Rosalind as adopted daughter for the murderously bad foster son Prince Hal.

But Shakespeare does not indulge fantasies; Hamlet and Falstaff must die. As compensation, we are offered, at least in *Hamlet*, perspectives that keep reminding us we sit in a theater, intensely conscious that Hamlet, despite his brilliance, is only his creator's puppet. The function of the gap Shakespeare cuts into *Hamlet* is to keep Hobgoblin from running off with the garland of Apollo. Faulconbridge in *King John*, and Shylock, had walked off with their plays. Mercutio had been killed by Shakespeare lest he did the same. To say of Falstaff that he makes off with the two parts of *Henry IV* would be weak understatement. Shakespeare had promised to bring Falstaff to France in *Henry V*, and sensibly thought better of it, killing the great wit to the gorgeous funeral music of Mistress Quickly's elegiac Cockney prose. No one, not even Shakespeare, could curtail Hamlet's largeness of being, but Shakespeare had the audacity to keep Hamlet under some control by immersing us in plays within plays within plays.

WHEN ROSENCRANTZ tells Hamlet that the players are "coming to offer you service," the prince answers,

"What players are they?" and is told, "Even those you were wont to take such delight in, the tragedians of the city." Manifestly, this is Shakespeare's own company, and Shakespeare's audience would have been in on the joke, as we cannot be now, without scholarly aid. The best I know is *Shakespeare and the Poets' War* (2001), by James P. Bednarz. Rosencrantz, doubtless to the delight of *Hamlet*'s audience, overstresses the discomfiting of Shakespeare and his company by Ben Jonson's Children of the Chapel, with whom Jonson worked in 1600–1601. Hamlet, surprised that Shakespeare's players have taken the road to Elsinore, demands explanation from Rosencrantz:

HAMLET *How chances it they travel? . . . Do they hold the same estimation they did when I was in the city? Are they so followed?*

ROSENCRANTZ *No, indeed are they not.*

HAMLET *How comes it? Do they grow rusty?*

ROSENCRANTZ *Nay, their endeavour keeps in the wonted pace; but there is, sir, an eyrie of children, little eyases, that cry out on the top of question, and are most tyrannically clapped for't. These are now the fashion, and so berattle the common stages—so they call them—*

that many wearing rapiers are afraid of goose-quills and dare scarce come thither.

HAMLET   *What, are they children? Who maintains 'em? How are they escotted? Will they pursue the quality no longer than they can sing? Will they not say afterwards, if they should grow themselves to common players—as it is most like, if their means are no better— their writers do them wrong to make them exclaim against their own succession?*

ROSENCRANTZ   *Faith, there has been much to do on both sides; and the nation holds it no sin to tar them to controversy. There was for a while no money bid for argument unless the poet and the player went to cuffs in the question.*

HAMLET   *Is't possible?*

GUILDENSTERN   *O, there has been much throwing about of brains.*

HAMLET   *Do the boys carry it away?*

ROSENCRANTZ   *Ay, that they do, my lord, Hercules and his load too.*

[II.ii.328–58]

The Globe audience, knowing that the globe was Hercules' load, would be roaring by now, appreciating

23

that Shakespeare's hyperbole was refuted by a packed house. The aerie of little eyases, a nest of young hawks, Jonson's child actors, were being compelled by surly Ben to "exclaim against their own succession," since maturing into adult actors was their only destiny. Bednarz expounds all this admirably. I wish to shift focus to this question: Why does Shakespeare, here and in what follows, so cheerfully hazard the dramatic continuity and persuasive power of *Hamlet*?

WE WILL not leave the world of players and plays until Hamlet stands poised, sword in hand, above the kneeling and praying Claudius (Act III, Scene iii, 70–96). By then, the prince has been perspectivized for us as being only the most substantial shadow on a stage of shadows. We are so mastered by Shakespeare (as we should be) that we rarely stop to reflect upon how bizarre Hamlet's story has become. Is it still a drama? Isn't Hamlet himself no more or less ghostly than his father? So powerfully has Hamlet impressed his creator, as well as ourselves, that he is asked to survive as a veritable apocalypse of theatricalities, heaped upon one another. After the hilarity of gossip on the Poets' War between Shakespeare

and Jonson, we are given Hamlet-as-Shakespeare, ad-
monishing and instructing the Globe's actors, and then
we go on to not one but two plays-within-plays, both
travesties of blood-melodrama. The first has no title,
but the second has two, *The Murder of Gonzago* and *The
Mousetrap*. The untitled bloody farce could be called
The Slaughter of Priam, with the Lamentation of Hecuba,
and is of a poetic badness not to be believed:

> *The rugged Pyrrhus, he whose sable arms,*
> *Black as his purpose, did the night resemble*
> *When he lay couched in the ominous horse,*
> *Hath now this dread and black complexion smear'd*
> *With heraldry more dismal. Head to foot*
> *Now is he total gules, horridly trick'd*
> *With blood of fathers, mothers, daughters, sons,*
> *Bak'd and impasted with the parching streets,*
> *That lend a tyrannous and damned light*
> *To their lord's murder. Roasted in wrath and fire,*
> *And thus o'ersized with coagulate gore,*
> *With eyes like carbuncles, the hellish Pyrrhus*
> *Old grandsire Priam seeks.*

[II.ii. 448–60]

Hamlet professes to admire this, and repeats it from memory, having experienced it at the supposed single performance of the play from which it is extracted, a play that never existed. Since Shakespeare's own *Troilus and Cressida* "was never acted, or if it was, not above once," Hamlet is treating us to another Shakespearean in-joke. Whatever the account of Priam's slaughter parodies, it is not *Troilus and Cressida* but some imaginary play Christopher Marlowe never survived to write. The First Player, or Player King, almost certainly the actor Will Shakespeare, then takes over, and gives us the rest of Pyrrhus's butchery of Priam, followed by Queen Hecuba's lament for her husband. Even as Marlovian parody, this surely would have irritated the Globe audience had Shakespeare not, with delicious irony, had Polonius protest, "This is too long," and Hamlet chide Polonius, "It shall to the barber's with your beard." Still funnier, after Hamlet urges the First Player to continue on with Hecuba, both the prince and the councilor of state force a pause after the line "But who—ah, woe!— had seen the mobbled queen—." Presumably a Shakespearean coinage, "mobbled" must mean that the poor lady had her face muffled. Hamlet, pretending to relish the touch, repeats, " 'The mobbled queen,' " and Polonius renders aesthetic judgment: "That's good." Thus encouraged, the First Player gives us a third swatch of verbiage, which allows Will the actor to turn red with passion and weep, doubtless captivating the Globe.

FOUR

TWO SOLILOQUIES

Hamlet sets the stage, so that the actor Richard Burbage can out-act Will Shakespeare, as the audience rightly expects. The First Player has come apart, "for Hecuba," and Hamlet spurs himself on to a more extraordinary performance:

> *What's Hecuba to him, or he to her,*
> *That he should weep for her? What would he do*
> *Had he the motive and the cue for passion*
> *That I have? He would drown the stage with tears,*
> *And cleave the general ear with horrid speech,*

Make mad the guilty and appal the free,
Confound the ignorant, and amaze indeed
The very faculties of eyes and ears.

[II.ii.553–60]

So histrionic is all of *Hamlet* that we need to develop our auditory consciousness to a new pitch, if we catch the prince's precise accent here. Where all is theatricality, our grounds for judgment must shift. Hamlet's hyperboles mock theater itself, in "drown the stage with tears." The soliloquy becomes a hyperparody of soliloquy, as Shakespeare allows Burbage to transcend Marlowe's roaring actor, Alleyn, who had played Tamburlaine the Great and the Jewish Machiavel, Barabas:

Yet I,
A dull and muddy-mettled rascal, peak
Like John-a-dreams, unpregnant of my cause,
And can say nothing—no, not for a king,
Upon whose property and most dear life
A damn'd defeat was made. Am I a coward?
Who calls me villain, breaks my pate across,
Plucks off my beard and blows it in my face,
Tweaks me by the nose, gives me the lie i'th' throat

As deep as to the lungs—who does me this?
Ha!
'Swounds, I should take it: for it cannot be
But I am pigeon-liver'd and lack gall
To make oppression bitter, or ere this
I should ha' fatted all the region kites
With this slave's offal. Bloody, bawdy villain!
Remorseless, treacherous, lecherous, kindless villain!

[II.ii.560–77]

When Hamlet is not whipping himself up, he imagines physical abuse from a censorious alter ego, but he is highly aware of his playacting. Once an intricate melder of language and the self, the prince has begun to disjoin them. His heavy irony is defensive, but cannot veil his conviction that his words whore him:

Why, what an ass am I! This is most brave,
That I, the son of a dear father murder'd,
Prompted to my revenge by heaven and hell,
Must like a whore unpack my heart with words
And fall a-cursing like a very drab,
A scullion! Fie upon't! Foh!

[II.ii.578–83]

What he intimates is larger and more lasting than his momentary self-disgust. If you can unpack your heart with words, then what you express is already dead within you. With no faith left in either language or the self, and no transcendental allegiances, Hamlet nevertheless retains a conviction in the truth-inducings of theater:

> *About, my brains. Hum——I have heard*
> *That guilty creatures sitting at a play*
> *Have, by the very cunning of the scene,*
> *Been struck so to the soul that presently*
> *They have proclaim'd their malefactions.*
> *For murder, though it have no tongue, will speak*
> *With most miraculous organ. I'll have these players*
> *Play something like the murder of my father*
> *Before mine uncle. I'll observe his looks;*
> *I'll tent him to the quick. If a do blench,*
> *I know my course. The spirit that I have seen*
> *May be a devil, and the devil hath power*
> *T'assume a pleasing shape, yea, and perhaps,*
> *Out of my weakness and my melancholy,*
> *As he is very potent with such spirits,*
> *Abuses me to damn me. I'll have grounds*

More relative than this. The play's the thing
Wherein I'll catch the conscience of the King.

[II.ii.584–601]

Since Hamlet has already requested the Player King
to play *The Murder of Gonzago,* with revisions by the
prince himself, his "About, my brains" is redundant.
But as his own best audience, Hamlet wants to play it
again, exalting "the very cunning of the scene." It is
doubtful that he thinks his father's spirit to be a devil,
but he wants the play. "The play's the thing" itself, his
true vocation.

ONLY FIFTY-FIVE lines later, the most illustrious
of all soliloquies begins Hamlet's next appearance. As
probably the most famous verse passage in the language,
staled by repetition, it challenges us to restore its authentic and perpetual freshness. Best to state baldly: This is
not a meditation seriously contemplating suicide:

To be, or not to be, that is the question:
Whether 'tis nobler in the mind to suffer

The slings and arrows of outrageous fortune,
Or to take arms against a sea of troubles
And by opposing end them. To die—to sleep,
No more; and by a sleep to say we end
The heart-ache and the thousand natural shocks
That flesh is heir to: 'tis a consummation
Devoutly to be wish'd. To die, to sleep;
To sleep, perchance to dream—ay, there's the rub:
For in that sleep of death what dreams may come,
When we have shuffled off this mortal coil,
Must give us pause—there's the respect
That makes calamity of so long life.
For who would bear the whips and scorns of time,
Th'oppressor's wrong, the proud man's contumely,
The pangs of dispriz'd love, the law's delay,
The insolence of office, and the spurns
That patient merit of th'unworthy takes,
When he himself might his quietus make
With a bare bodkin? Who would fardels bear,
To grunt and sweat under a weary life,
But that the dread of something after death,
The undiscover'd country, from whose bourn
No traveller returns, puzzles the will,
And makes us rather bear those ills we have

Than fly to others that we know not of?
Thus conscience does make cowards of us all,
And thus the native hue of resolution
Is sicklied o'er with the pale cast of thought,
And enterprises of great pitch and moment
With this regard their currents turn awry
And lose the name of action.

[III.i.56–88]

What is the power of Hamlet's mind over a universe of death, or a sea of troubles? That indeed is the question. Shakespeare's heirs, from Milton through Wordsworth to Wallace Stevens, have explored this question incessantly, for this has become the burden of post-Enlightenment poetry. The sea of death, representative of mother night, must end consciousness—or "conscience," in Hamlet's term. But how far, before that, does the power of the poet's mind extend?

Being, or consciousness, is given the choice: suffer stoically, or take arms against the sea, and thus end sooner, consumed by the currents, whose great pitch constitutes a height our enterprises cannot attain. There are two grand metaphors in conflict here: the shuffled-off mortal coil, everything we shall lose, and the undiscovered country, the land of death, from which no traveler returns, yet from which King Hamlet's spirit breaks loose twice in the play. The spirit seeks revenge, and it comes, though not through Prince Hamlet's will.

And yet the prince's mind, though it cannot prevail over the universe of death, sets the standard by which Milton, Wordsworth, and Stevens will measure the extent of their own power over outward sense. Hamlet's will loses the *name* of action, but not the true nature of action, which abides in the exaltation of mind. It can be objected: Where is there such exaltation in this soliloquy? And the answer is: Everywhere, in each phrase, in each pause, as this grandest of consciousnesses overhears its own cognitive music.

FIVE

OPHELIA

We first encounter Ophelia in a familial context, with her departing brother Laertes and her father Polonius alike warning her not to yield her person to Hamlet. "I shall obey, my lord," she gently says to her father, and so her tragedy already is in place. Shakespeare, whose art is elliptical, even in this richest and most various of his plays, does not dramatize the scene between Hamlet and Ophelia where the prince first experiments with putting an antic disposition on, but allows Ophelia to narrate:

He took me by the wrist and held me hard.
Then goes he to the length of all his arm,
And with his other hand thus o'er his brow
He falls to such perusal of my face
As a would draw it. Long stay'd he so.
At last, a little shaking of mine arm,
And thrice his head thus waving up and down,
He rais'd a sigh so piteous and profound
As it did seem to shatter all his bulk
And end his being. That done, he lets me go,
And with his head over his shoulders turn'd
He seem'd to find his way without his eyes,
For out o' doors he went without their helps,
And to the last bended their light on me.

[II.i.88–100]

What emerges clearly is that Hamlet is playacting, and that Ophelia already is the prime victim of his dissembling. John Ruskin, meditating upon Shakespeare's names, sensitively commented:

Ophelia, "serviceableness," the true lost wife of Ham-
let, is marked by having a Greek name by that of her

brother, Laertes; and its signification is once exquisitely
alluded to in that brother's last word of her, where her
gentle preciousness is opposed to the uselessness of the
churlish clergy—"a ministering *angel shall my sister*
be, when thou liest howling."

Between Hamlet's "To be or not to be" soliloquy
and his Shakespeare-like instructing of the players,
we are given the prince's astonishingly brutal verbal
assault upon Ophelia, which far surpasses his need to
persuade the concealed Claudius of his nephew's supposed madness. What broader ambivalence Hamlet har-
bors toward Ophelia, Shakespeare will not tell us,
but neither Polonius's exploitation of his daughter as
unwitting spy, nor Hamlet's association of Ophelia with
Gertrude, can account for the vehemence of this denun-
ciation:

HAMLET *Get thee to a nunnery. Why, wouldst thou be*
a breeder of sinners? I am myself indifferent honest, but
yet I could accuse me of such things that it were better
my mother had not borne me. I am very proud, revenge-
ful, ambitious, with more offences at my beck than I

have thoughts to put them in, imagination to give them shape, or time to act them in. What should such fellows as I do crawling between earth and heaven? We are arrant knaves all, believe none of us. Go thy ways to a nunnery. Where's your father?

OPHELIA   *At home, my lord.*

HAMLET   *Let the doors be shut upon him, that he may play the fool nowhere but in's own house. Farewell.*

OPHELIA   *O help him, you sweet heavens.*

HAMLET   *If thou dost marry, I'll give thee this plague for thy dowry: be thou as chaste as ice, as pure as snow, thou shalt not escape calumny. Get thee to a nunnery, farewell. Or if thou wilt needs marry, marry a fool; for wise men know well enough what monsters you make of them. To a nunnery, go—and quickly too. Farewell.*

OPHELIA   *Heavenly powers, restore him.*

HAMLET   *I have heard of your paintings well enough. God hath given you one face and you make yourselves another. You jig and amble, and you lisp, you nickname God's creatures, and make your wantonness your ignorance. Go to, I'll no more on't, it hath made me mad. I say we will have no mo marriage. Those that are mar-*

ried already—all but one—shall live; the rest shall keep as they are. To a nunnery, go.

[III.i.121–51]

There are overtones here of the slang meaning of "nunnery" as "whorehouse," but primarily Hamlet consigns Ophelia to a life of pious chastity. Yet in effect, he is murdering Ophelia, and starting her on the path to suicide. One hesitates to say this is Hamlet's least sympathetic moment in the play. His blithe unconcern after slaughtering Polonius ("I'll lug the guts into the neighbour room") would be another candidate, as would his gratuitous destruction of those interchangeable scamps Rosencrantz and Guildenstern:

HORATIO *So Guildenstern and Rosencrantz go to't.*
HAMLET *Why, man, they did make love to this employment.*
They are not near my conscience, their defeat
Does by their own insinuation grow.
'Tis dangerous when the baser nature comes
Between the pass and fell incensed points
Of mighty opposites.

[V.ii.56–62]

Horatio presumably expresses shock, and some regret, but Hamlet shrugs off the pragmatic murder of his two school chums. Polonius is an old meddler, and Guildenstern and Rosencrantz are confidence men at best, but the fragile and lovely Ophelia is quite another matter, and Hamlet is monstrous to torment her into true madness. One of Shakespeare's great set pieces, Gertrude's description of Ophelia's suicide, gives the play a lyrical splendor that helps justify Dr. Johnson's praise of its variety:

> QUEEN *There is a willow grows askant the brook*
> *That shows his hoary leaves in the glassy stream.*
> *Therewith fantastic garlands did she make*
> *Of crow-flowers, nettles, daisies, and long purples,*
> *That liberal shepherds give a grosser name,*
> *But our cold maids do dead men's fingers call them.*
> *There on the pendent boughs her crownet weeds*
> *Clamb'ring to hang, an envious sliver broke,*
> *When down her weedy trophies and herself*
> *Fell in the weeping brook. Her clothes spread wide,*
> *And mermaid-like awhile they bore her up,*
> *Which time she chanted snatches of old lauds,*

As one incapable of her own distress,
Or like a creature native and indued
Unto that element. But long it could not be
Till that her garments, heavy with their drink,
Pull'd the poor wretch from her melodious lay
To muddy death.

LAERTES   *Alas, then she is drown'd.*
GERTRUDE   *Drown'd, drown'd.*

[IV.vii.165–83]

The pathos here yields to an extraordinary aesthetic effect, unique to Ophelia. The contrast between "muddy death" and the vision of the mad girl singing songs of praises as she floats has a sublime resonance, akin to Hamlet's realization that he is at once nothing and everything in himself, "infinite in faculties," and "this quintessence of dust." The loving Ophelia, a "ministering angel," dies chanting as an image less of victimization than of the power of Shakespeare's language to evoke a unique beauty.

That beauty is engendered by Hamlet's cruelty, indeed by his failure to love. Despite his passion in the graveyard, we have every reason to doubt his capacity to love anyone, even Ophelia. He does not want or need love: that is his lonely freedom, and it provokes the audience's unreasoning affection for him. Shakespeare's wisdom avoided the only fate for Ophelia that would have been more plangent than her death-in-water: marriage to Hamlet the Dane.

SIX

SHAKESPEARE
TO THE PLAYERS

Act III, Scene ii, begins with forty-five lines in which Hamlet instructs and admonishes three of the players who are to enact his *Mousetrap*. In this poem unlimited of so many wonders, nothing is more central than Hamlet's excursus upon the purpose of playing. Only the First Player, who will act the Player King, is allowed any replies, and these are confined to "I warrant your honour" and "I hope we have reformed that indifferently with us." That is the player Will Shakespeare meekly accepting the authority of the player Richard

Burbage, who transparently speaks not as the prince of Denmark but as the resident dramatist of the Globe. Something of the high good humor of this, four centuries ago at the Globe, necessarily is lost to us now. Yet the gain is larger than the loss, since we long to listen to Shakespeare's own voice and rarely are offered it, even in the Sonnets. Now we hear it:

> *Speak the speech, I pray you, as I pronounced it to you, trippingly on the tongue; but if you mouth it as many of your players do, I had as lief the town-crier spoke my lines. Nor do not saw the air too much with your hand, thus, but use all gently; for in the very torrent, tempest, and, as I may say, whirlwind of your passion, you must acquire and beget a temperance that may give it smoothness. O, it offends me to the soul to hear a robustious periwig-pated fellow tear a passion to tatters, to very rags, to split the ears of the groundlings, who for the most part are capable of nothing but inexplicable dumb-shows and noise. I would have such a fellow whipped for o'erdoing Termagant, It out-Herods Herod. Pray you avoid it.*

> [III.ii.1–14]

The overactor, or roaring boy, is to imitate Shakespeare-Hamlet, who has just spoken, trippingly on the tongue, what I take to be the speech of the Player King, still too little valued by our critics and directors:

PLAYER KING   *I do believe you think what now you speak;*
But what we do determine, oft we break.
Purpose is but the slave to memory,
Of violent birth but poor validity,
Which now, the fruit unripe, sticks on the tree,
But fall unshaken when they mellow be.
Most necessary 'tis that we forget
To pay ourselves what to ourselves is debt.
What to ourselves in passion we propose,
The passion ending, doth the purpose lose.
The violence of either grief or joy
Their own enactures with themselves destroy.
Where joy most revels grief doth most lament;
Grief joys, joy grieves, on slender accident.
This world is not for aye, nor 'tis not strange
That even our loves should with our fortunes change,
For 'tis a question left us yet to prove,

Whether love lead fortune or else fortune love.
The great man down, you mark his favourite flies;
The poor advanc'd makes friends of enemies;
And hitherto doth love on fortune tend:
For who not needs shall never lack a friend,
And who in want a hollow friend doth try
Directly seasons him his enemy.
But orderly to end where I begun,
Our wills and fates do so contrary run
That our devices still are overthrown:
Our thoughts are ours, their ends none of our own.

[III.ii.181–208]

Whose nature is mirrored here, Hamlet's or human-kind's? Do all of us will against our own characters/fates, so that our designs always are thwarted? If character is fate, so that there are no accidents, then our desires do not matter. Freud thought it was all over before our first birthday; Hamlet seems to give us even less freedom from overdetermination. If everything that ever will happen to you is only a mirror of your own character, then holding the mirror up to nature becomes rather a dark activity: all of us are the fools of time, victims of an unfolding we cannot affect. I do not think that this is Shakespeare's own vision, nor will it be Hamlet's, in Act V, yet it is evidently Hamlet's ground of despair in the life he has endured before his return from the sea. When we see him in the graveyard, in Act V, he will have been resurrected.

SEVEN

THE MOUSETRAP:
CONTRARY WILL

Hamlet's own nature never can be confined to a single purpose, but a mousetrap has only one function. In Act V, Hamlet becomes the freest artist of himself in all literature, yet in the abyss of Act II, Scene ii, through Act III, Scene vi, all artistry is put to the question. Are we spectators at a play, or are we the play? "The players cannot keep counsel: they'll tell all," Hamlet remarks to Ophelia. But can we, under Shakespeare's influence, still keep counsel? Rightfully hurt, Ophelia tells Hamlet, "You are as good as a chorus, my lord." There is an implied reproach: the chorus is not a protagonist. With fierce wit, Hamlet replies, "I could interpret between you and your love if I could see the puppets dallying." Ophelia has no other love: Hamlet would be spectator to his own dalliance. The copulating puppets have no voice without the interpreter. Oscar Wilde, interpreting the enormous influence of *Hamlet,* remarked that the world has grown melancholy because a puppet, the prince, was sad. *The Mousetrap* is a puppet show, but so is *Hamlet,* at least until the end of Act IV.

Wilde argued that nature held a mirror up to playing, a contention echoed by W. B. Yeats, for whom mirror upon mirror was all the scene. Hamlet, however generally melancholy, is never more exuberantly cheerful than when Claudius rises, "frighted with false fire," and rushes out shouting: "Give me some light. Away." In the pride of having made a better mousetrap, Hamlet claims Shakespeare's own share in the Globe's proceeds:

> HAMLET   *Would not this, sir, and a forest of feathers,*
> *if the rest of my fortunes turn Turk with me, with Provin-*
> *cial roses on my razed shoes, get me a fellowship in a cry*
> *of players?*

HORATIO   *Half a share.*
HAMLET   *A whole one, I.*
       [III.ii.269–72]

Could not *The Tragedy of Hamlet, Prince of Denmark,* be retitled *A Cry of Players?* What possesses Shakespeare to drive him on in this pack of theatricalities? Richard Lanham, rhetorically more than aware that Shakespeare is "writing a play about the kind of play he is writing," brilliantly echoes Hamlet: "Human flesh is sullied with self-consciousness, with theatricality." Yes, but no other human (or puppet, if you prefer) is as sullied as Hamlet. Shakespeare's theatricalism is there in all the plays, but nowhere else is it as aggressive as in *Hamlet.* Why? The prince, if we press him too close on this, is likely to compound us with the cat's-paw Guildenstern:

Why, look you now, how unworthy a thing you make of me. You would play upon me, you would seem to know my stops, you would pluck out the heart of my mystery, you would sound me from my lowest note to the top of my compass; and there is much music, excellent voice, in this little organ, yet cannot you make it speak.

'Sblood, do you think I am easier to be played on than a pipe? Call me what instrument you will, though you fret me, you cannot play upon me.

[III.ii.354–63]

We cannot play upon him: he is cleverer than we are, and more dangerous. But for the Ghost's second appearance, we wonder if Hamlet *would* murder Gertrude, as Nero executed his mother, Agrippina, who had poisoned her husband, another Claudius. Hamlet duly warns himself against just this, but only after disclaiming, "Now could I drink hot blood." He is sufficiently rough with her to cause the outcry "What wilt thou do? Thou wilt not murder me?" In the event, he assuages his rage by manslaughter, skewering Polonius through a curtain, but the thrust is a displacement of his true will, which is to immolate Gertrude.

Despite the urgings of Freud, and of his hagiographer Ernest Jones, there are no traces of Oedipus in Hamlet. The Hamlet Complex is not incestuous but again theatrical. Hamlet, prince of players, kills players; at the tragedy's close we are richer by eight corpses: Claudius, Gertrude, Polonius, Laertes, Ophelia, Rosencrantz, Guildenstern, and Hamlet himself. The stage is bare except for Horatio and Fortinbras, and a bevy of spear carriers, and since Horatio attempts suicide, we might almost have been down to one, the killing machine Fortinbras. That is prodigal even for Shakespearean tragedy, but belongs to the Hamlet Complex, of which murderousness forms as large a component as does self-conscious theatricality. Or are the two components fused: should we speak of a murderous theatricalism?

Shakespeare's first tragedy, *Titus Andronicus,* no matter what its defenders say, is palpably a bloody farce, a send-up of Marlowe and Kyd. *Hamlet* is anything but that, yet the glint in the eye of the maker of *Titus Andronicus* isn't altogether extinguished in *Hamlet.* What Hazlitt called gusto is the play's salient characteristic. Hamlet is so exuberant, whether in irony or grief, that his rhetorical excessiveness rivals Falstaff's. Falstaff, bless him and us, is not at all murderous: he rightly ascribes blood-madness to "honor," and he will have none of it. We can be reasonably certain that Shakespeare shared more of Falstaff's spirit than of Hamlet's. The speaker of the Sonnets has no will to hurt anyone, whatever the provocation. If compelled to march into battle, he would have emulated Falstaff, and taken along a bottle of sherris-sack in his holster.

Falstaff, master of theater, nevertheless is scarcely theatrical. Sir John need not play the part of Falstaff: he is neither a double man nor a counterfeit. Hamlet is a multiple man: who can count him? He *says* that he counterfeits madness, and I believe him, but how much else does he counterfeit?

Some critics believe Hamlet when he complains that he is caught up in a play not at all suitable for him. I once believed that, but now I rather doubt that we ought to give credence to Hamlet, because he is his own Iago as well as his own Falstaff.

EIGHT

GERTRUDE

There is a recent "Be kind to Gertrude" fashion among some feminist critics, though only John Updike (so far as I know) has extended the defense to Claudius. It is difficult not to be attracted by Gertrude, because Shakespeare has endowed her with an amiable lustiness. Hamlet is magnificently eloquent but other-wise badly self-advised when he admonishes his mother and denounces her healthy appetite:

> *You cannot call it love; for at your age*
> *The heyday in the blood is tame, it's humble,*

And waits upon the judgment, and what judgment
Would step from this to this? Sense sure you have,
Else could you not have motion; but sure that sense
Is apoplex'd, for madness would not err
Nor sense to ecstasy was ne'er so thrall'd
But it reserv'd some quantity of choice
To serve in such a difference. What devil was't
That this hath cozen'd you at hoodman-blind?
Eyes without feeling, feeling without sight,
Ears without hands or eyes, smelling sans all,
Or but a sickly part of one true sense
Could not so mope. O shame, where is thy blush?

[III.iv.68–81]

T. S. Eliot, who had his own aversion toward his mother, particularly admired (and imitated) the most piercing lines here:

Eyes without feeling, feeling without sight,
Ears without hands or eyes . . .

Gertrude needs defending only if she knew that Claudius had poisoned King Hamlet, and nothing in the text indicates that. Shakespeare does not resolve the enigma of how far back the relationship with Claudius goes, but I think we can assume that Gertrude required some solace whenever the warlike King Hamlet was off slaying the first Fortinbras or smiting the sledded Polacks on the ice. That surmised, Gertrude and Claudius certainly are one of the happiest marriages in Shakespeare until the Ghost sets young Hamlet upon his very hesitant quest for revenge. Still, I would vote for the Macbeths as much the best marriage in Shakespeare, so the connubial bliss of Gertrude and Claudius is somewhat irrelevant, once murder outs.

Prince Hamlet is not exactly one of Shakespeare's most loving characters, though he protests otherwise. Ophelia evidently dies a virgin, though Hamlet would seem to have garnered experience elsewhere, to judge from his general knowingness and his theatrical connections. He is conversant with Shakespeare's players, and the Globe was hardly a temple of chastity. Aldous Huxley's useful formula—"high brows, low loins"—can be invoked in regard to the best mind ever represented in literature.

Shakespeare, as is customary with his superb perspectivism, does not allow Hamlet to mediate Gertrude for us. That is certainly a gain, since Hamlet carries his grudge to the grave. After Gertrude dies, calling out, "O my dear Hamlet!" her son delivers the extraordinary line "I am dead, Horatio. Wretched Queen, adieu." One feels that as heroic a sexuality as Gertrude's deserves some warmth in a final salutation; she should have mothered Falstaff rather than Hamlet.

We remember Gertrude for two scenes in particular: her narration of Ophelia's death by water, and her terrified response to her authentically frightening son in the closet and portrait confrontation. Gertrude's is a challenging role for an actress, and I have seen only a few good performances of the part. But then, how difficult it is to play any role in Hamlet's tragedy, where the actor attempting the crucial consciousness is given three-eighths of the lines, and is almost always the center of concern, even when he is offstage. Falstaff, Iago, and Cleopatra do not have mothers (or fathers, either), and only they and Lear rival Hamlet as representations. Gertrude had much to endure, and little to enjoy, in her brilliant son.

NINE

CLAUDIUS

Hamlet, having sent Guildenstern and Rosencrantz off to an English beheading, shrugs off his culpability:

> *'Tis dangerous when the baser nature comes*
> *Between the pass and fell incensed points*
> *Of mighty opposites.*

> [V.ii.60–62]

If Shakespeare really intended the shuffling Claudius as Hamlet's "mighty opposite," then he blundered, since the typical exchange between uncle and nephew tends to turn the exasperated usurper into a hysteric. I give a long but marvelous instance:

KING   *Now, Hamlet, where's Polonius?*

HAMLET   *At supper.*

KING   *At supper? Where?*

HAMLET   *Not where he eats, but where a is eaten. A certain convocation of politic worms are e'en at him. Your worm is your only emperor for diet: we fat all creatures else to fat us, and we fat ourselves for maggots. Your fat king and your lean beggar is but variable service—two dishes, but to one table. That's the end.*

KING   *Alas, alas.*

HAMLET   *A man may fish with the worm that hath eat of a king, and eat of the fish that hath fed of that worm.*

KING   *What dost thou mean by this?*

HAMLET   *Nothing but to show you how a king may go a progress through the guts of a beggar.*

KING   *Where is Polonius?*

HAMLET   *In heaven. Send thither to see. If your messenger find him not there, seek him i'th' other place yourself. But if indeed you find him not within this*

month, *you shall nose him as you go up the stairs into
the lobby.*

KING   [To some attendants] *Go seek him there.*

HAMLET   *A will stay till you come.*   [Exeunt atten-
dants.]

KING   *Hamlet, this deed, for thine especial safety—
Which we do tender, as we dearly grieve
For that which thou hast done—must send thee hence
With fiery quickness. Therefore prepare thyself.
The bark is ready, and the wind at help,
Th'associates tend, and everything is bent
For England.*

HAMLET   *For England?*

KING   *Ay, Hamlet.*

HAMLET   *Good.*

KING   *So is it, if thou knew'st our purposes.*

HAMLET   *I see a cherub that sees them. But come, for
England. Farewell, dear mother.*

KING   *Thy loving father, Hamlet.*

HAMLET   *My mother. Father and mother is man and
wife, man and wife is one flesh; so my mother. Come,
for England.*

[Exit.]

[IV.iii.16–55]

It is palpable that Claudius is a minor-league rhetorician confronting an all-time all-star, and that Shakespeare realizes he has only a puny opposite for the prince. Claudius's absurd slip "So is it, if thou knew'st our purposes" invites the crusher "I see a cherub that sees them." Until that, we have high hilarity, with the bewildered Claudius as the butt. Hamlet is so deliciously outrageous that we forgive his slaughter of Polonius, a politic worm now the center of a convocation of his peers. Claudius, always off balance, attempts to recoup with the setup of Laertes and the poisoned rapier, and a poisoned chalice as backup. If Claudius is only a minor-league Machiavel, Laertes isn't even that, but just an amateur assassin. Their plot, absurd and messy, would fool no one except that the Hamlet of Act V wishes to make an end, and will accept any Claudian wager, whatever the odds.

But why should Shakespeare have burdened us with mere Claudius as Hamlet's foeman? A. C. Bradley gives us the clue when he fantasizes an encounter between Hamlet and Iago, in which the prince would see through Iago in a moment and then drive the Satanic villain to suicide by incessant satire and ironic mockery. Edmund of *King Lear* would do no better, nor would any other Shakespearean negation. Hamlet is the most formidable ironist ever to walk upon a stage, and Shakespeare is well aware of this. When the prince speaks of "mighty opposites," he is only being wistful.

TEN

THE IMPOSTUME

On his way to England, conveyed by the doomed Rosencrantz and Guildenstern, Hamlet encounters the captain from Fortinbras's army who has the task of informing Claudius that the Norwegian force is marching across Denmark (with permission) in order to have at the Poles. The expedition is to gain a worthless plot of ground, and prompts Hamlet to a wonderful outburst:

> *Two thousand souls and twenty thousand ducats*
> *Will not debate the question of this straw!*

> *This is the impostume of much wealth and peace,*
> *That inward breaks, and shows no cause without*
> *Why the man dies.*

> [IV.iv.25–29]

An abscess or cyst that breaks inwardly: at once this is societal, and an event in Hamlet's consciousness. G. K. Chesterton liked to say that Chaucer's irony was too large to be seen. Hamlet's irony is visible (not because it lacks immensity), but it is too varied to be categorized as rhetorical irony. His soliloquy spurred by the impostume is the last time we hear Hamlet in Act IV, and already he has intimations of the different stance he will assume in Act V. Of his seven soliloquies, this is the most complex:

> *How all occasions do inform against me,*
> *And spur my dull revenge. What is a man*
> *If his chief good and market of his time*
> *Be but to sleep and feed? A beast, no more.*
> *Sure he that made us with such large discourse,*
> *Looking before and after, gave us not*
> *That capability and godlike reason*
> *To fust in us unus'd. Now whether it be*

Bestial oblivion, or some craven scruple
Of thinking too precisely on th'event—
A thought which, quarter'd, hath but one part wisdom
And ever three parts coward—I do not know
Why yet I live to say this thing's to do,
Sith I have cause, and will, and strength, and means
To do't. Examples gross as earth exhort me,
Witness this army of such mass and charge,
Led by a delicate and tender prince,
Whose spirit, with divine ambition puff'd,
Makes mouths at the invisible event,
Exposing what is mortal and unsure
To all that fortune, death, and danger dare,
Even for an eggshell. Rightly to be great
Is not to stir without great argument,
But greatly to find quarrel in a straw
When honour's at the stake. How stand I then,
That have a father kill'd, a mother stain'd,
Excitements of my reason and my blood,
And let all sleep, while to my shame I see
The imminent death of twenty thousand men
That, for a fantasy and trick of fame,
Go to their graves like beds, fight for a plot
Whereon the numbers cannot try the cause,

Which is not tomb enough and continent
To hide the slain? O, from this time forth
My thoughts be bloody or be nothing worth.

[IV.iv.32–66]

When he returns from the sea, his thoughts will be anything but bloody. Yet he is no longer bloody-minded here, despite his self-exhortings. Are we not at the precise moment where his theatricalism and his inwardness break from each other? Vastly intelligent, far beyond us—if we are not, say, Freud or Wittgenstein—Hamlet cannot believe that the proper use of his capability and godlike reason is to perform a revenge killing. In truth, he has no desire to cut down Claudius, which is not an action that requires Hamletian powers of awareness. The disproportion between agent and act could have been masked only by theatricalism, and honor is not mask enough to convert an eggshell, like Claudius, into a great argument. Hamlet's impostume is the absurdity of accommodating his greatness to the rotten state of Denmark. Prince Hal, breaking from Falstaff, becomes Henry IV's avenger, only in the sense that conquering France masks Henry IV's murder and usurpation of his cousin, Richard II. Hamlet is not Hal: only fusing Falstaff and Hal together could you achieve some version of Hamlet, and perhaps that is what Shakespeare had some thought of doing. But Shakespeare's theatrical defense against Hamlet's unlimitedness has begun to waver, and will be overwhelmed in Act V.

Is *The Tragedy of Hamlet, Prince of Denmark* Shakespeare's impostume? The break into inwardness was unsurpassable, and made possible Iago, Othello, Lear, Edmund, Edgar, Macbeth, Cleopatra, Antony, an eightfold whose paths to the abyss were charted by Hamlet, death's ambassador to us. G. Wilson Knight first called *Hamlet* the embassy of death, and once remarked to me that he himself could confront the play only because of his strong belief in immortality. We do not know what Shakespeare believed about the soul's survival. Before Act V, Hamlet is confident of his soul's immortality, but I think he is different after his return from the sea, and I suspect he courts annihilation. When the impostume breaks, the man dies, and perhaps the soul with him, for in Hamlet consciousness and the soul have become one.

ELEVEN

THE GRAVE-DIGGER

We can assume that Robert Armin, who had replaced Will Kempe as Shakespeare's star clown, played the Grave-digger, whose part extends from his question concerning Ophelia's burial, at the start of Act V, through his laconic identification of Yorick's skull—"E'en that"— one hundred seventy-seven lines later. Hamlet's third speech to the players clearly had indicated Kempe, notorious for his jigs, stage business, and improvisations:

> *And let those that play your clowns speak no more than*
> *is set down for them—for there be of them that will*

themselves laugh, to set on some quantity of barren
spectators to laugh too, though in the meantime some
necessary question of the play be then to be considered.
That's villainous, and shows a most pitiful ambition in
the fool that uses it.

[III.ii.38–45]

The Grave-digger belongs to the triad of Shakespearean roles that also include the Porter in the knocking-at-
the-gate scene just after Duncan's murder in *Macbeth*,
and the countryman who sells Cleopatra the asps before her apotheosis-death. All three are remarkable set
pieces for a great clown like Robert Armin. I love the
Grave-digger best, because, as Hamlet remarks, he is so
"absolute," a positivist who insists upon strict interpre-
tations. He possesses also a chilling pride in his labor:

GRAVE-DIGGER *There is no ancient gentlemen but*
gardeners, ditchers, and grave-makers—they hold up
Adam's profession. [He digs.]
OTHER *Was he a gentleman?*
GRAVE-DIGGER *A was the first that ever bore arms.*
OTHER *Why, he had none.*
GRAVE-DIGGER *What, art a heathen? How dost thou*
understand the Scripture? The Scripture says Adam

digged. Could he dig without arms? I'll put another question to thee. If thou answerest me not to the purpose, confess thyself—

OTHER   *Go to.*

GRAVE-DIGGER   *What is he that builds stronger than either the mason, the shipwright, or the carpenter?*

OTHER   *The gallows-maker, for that frame outlives a thousand tenants.*

GRAVE-DIGGER   *I like thy wit well in good faith, the gallows does well. But how does it well? It does well to those that do ill. Now, thou dost ill to say the gallows is built stronger than the church; argal, the gallows may do well to thee. To't again, come.*

OTHER   *Who builds stronger than a mason, a shipwright, or a carpenter?*

GRAVE-DIGGER   *Ay, tell me that and unyoke.*

OTHER   *Marry, now I can tell.*

GRAVE-DIGGER   *To't.*

OTHER   *Mass, I cannot tell.*

GRAVE-DIGGER   *Cudgel thy brains no more about it, for your dull ass will not mend his pace with beating. And when you are asked this question next, say 'A grave-maker.' The houses he makes last till doomsday.*

[V.1.29–59]

The Grave-digger is the Old Adam, and his work will last till doomsday. His confrontation with the New Adam, Hamlet, finds him equal in dark wit to the formidable prince:

> HAMLET *How long will a man lie i'th' earth ere he rot?*
> GRAVE-DIGGER *Faith, if a be not rotten before a die—*
> *as we have many pocky corses nowadays that will scarce*
> *hold the laying in—a will last you some eight year or*
> *nine year. A tanner will last you nine year.*
> HAMLET *Why he more than another?*
> GRAVE-DIGGER *Why, sir, his hide is so tanned with*
> *his trade that a will keep out water a great while, and*
> *your water is a sore decayer of your whoreson dead body.*
> [V.i.158–66]

The Grave-digger is the reality principle, mortality, while Hamlet is death's scholar. Shakespeare sets Hamlet's death, in the Court, at Elsinore. By then, however, Hamlet long has seemed posthumous.

TWELVE

WONDER-WOUNDED

HEARERS

Shakespeare's pride in Hamlet's scandalous eloquence hardly could be more deliberately manifested than in the contrast with Laertes' fustian rhetoric:

LAERTES   *O, treble woe*
Fall ten times treble on that cursed head
Whose wicked deed thy most ingenious sense
Depriv'd thee of.——Hold off the earth awhile,
Till I have caught her once more in mine arms.

                              [Leaps in the grave.]
Now pile your dust upon the quick and dead,

Till of this flat a mountain you have made
T'o'ertop old Pelion or the skyish head
Of blue Olympus.

HAMLET   *What is he whose grief*
Bears such an emphasis, whose phrase of sorrow
Conjures the wand'ring stars and makes them stand
Like wonder-wounded hearers? This is I,
Hamlet the Dane.

LAERTES   [Grappling with him] *The devil take thy*
soul!

HAMLET   *Thou pray'st not well.*
I prithee take thy fingers from my throat,
For though I am not splenative and rash,
Yet have I in me something dangerous,
Which let thy wiseness fear. Hold off thy hand.

[V.i.239–56]

We are to envision the furious Laertes scrambling up
out of the grave, rather than Hamlet leaping into it.
Never more memorable, the Dane himself is also never
more dangerous, though powerfully controlled, in language and in the potential of deferred action. And of
course it is Hamlet (who in calling himself the Dane
directly challenges Claudius) who conjures the audience

so that we become wounded by wonder at the sea change in this great personage. We need not believe him, now or before, when he tells us he loved Ophelia, but we are delighted at his satire upon Laertes' bad verse:

> 'Swounds, show me what thou't do.
> Woo't weep, woo't fight, woo't fast, woo't tear thyself,
> Woo't drink up eisel, eat a crocodile?
> I'll do't. Dost come here to whine,
> To outface me with leaping in her grave?
> Be buried quick with her, and so will I.
> And if thou prate of mountains, let them throw
> Millions of acres on us, till our ground,
> Singeing his pate against the burning zone,
> Make Ossa like a wart. Nay, and thou'lt mouth,
> I'll rant as well as thou.

[V.i.274–84]

Who in Shakespeare could confront this Hamlet: not Iago, perhaps Cleopatra, certainly Sir John Falstaff, whose powers of irony and of diction would hold the prince off, if we were to suppose that Falstaff would not be more interested in a diversion to steal the scene. Anthony Burgess, in a later short story, had Shakespeare overgo Cervantes by staging a *Hamlet* with Falstaff assigned a role. I long to hear Falstaff's rejoinder to "Woo't drink up eisel [vinegar], eat a crocodile?" Yet this is the last moment when even Burgess's Shakespeare could introduce Sir John into Hamlet's tragedy. Once out of the graveyard, Act V becomes the play of Hamlet the Dane, whom we scarcely have encountered before.

THIRTEEN

IN MY HEART
THERE WAS A KIND
OF FIGHTING

HAMLET   *So much for this, sir. Now shall you see the
other.*

You do remember all the circumstances?

HORATIO   *Remember it, my lord!*

HAMLET   *Sir, in my heart there was a kind of fighting
That would not let me sleep. Methought I lay
Worse than the mutines in the bilboes. Rashly—
And prais'd be rashness for it: let us know
Our indiscretion sometime serves us well
When our deep plots do pall; and that should learn us
There's a divinity that shapes our ends,*

Rough-hew them how we will—
HORATIO *That is most certain.*

[V.II.I–I2]

I am not clear as to exactly what Horatio means in saying, "That is most certain," but I think he mistakes Hamlet's emphasis. The divinity, unnamed, seems neither Protestant nor Catholic, and may be hermetist rather than Christian. Much depends upon how you interpret "ends": as intentions, or consequences? Hamlet echoes the Player King: "Our thoughts are ours, their ends none of our own." The divinity may be one's own lost godhood, fallen into the world of love and sleep, and manifested now as one's genius, hewing finer than one's will can.

The prince, sleepless on the voyage to England, manifests his skills as pickpocket and forger, extracting his own death warrant from the sleeping Rosencrantz and Guildenstern, and then altering Claudius's murderous commission so that his wretched classmates will be beheaded by the English, at the supposed request of the Danish king. His account of this exploit has in it a remarkably unmixed pleasure of high theatricality:

Or I could make a prologue to my brains,
They had begun the play—

[V.ii.30–31]

This exuberance is carried by him through his teasing of the fop Osric and on into the duel, which he has anticipated on the voyage. In what spirit does the sea change ensue? One tries different terms—disinterested, quietistic, nihilistic—but none of them is sufficiently exact. Perhaps Shakespeare, having reinvented the human, transcended himself with a new kind of man, represented by Hamlet when he returns from the sea. The biblical new kind of man is King David, ancestor of Jesus, and the model for the chivalric ideal. The new Hamlet is the Danish (and English) David, come to confer his charisma as an image for our meditation.

FOURTEEN

WE DEFY AUGURY

Why does Hamlet consent to enter Claudius's murderous mousetrap, the poisoned duel with Laertes? The question opens again into the larger enigma: Why does Hamlet the Dane return to Elsinore, evidently with no plans to depose or execute his usurping uncle? The shuffling Claudius is bound to act: had the duel not snuffed out Hamlet, a dozen further schemes would have followed. Detachment toward his dilemma is all but absolute in the new Hamlet: "We defy augury." Defiance is scarcely detachment, but Hamlet's defiance is not easy to characterize.

So fierce is the prince's wit, advanced beyond even his prior brilliance, that it can obscure the audacity of his reentry into the Danish court. By returning, he has no options beyond killing or being killed. The same mob that followed Laertes could more readily be summoned by the prince, beloved of the people, according to Claudius's earlier, rueful admission. Yet Hamlet entertains no such prospects. Power is there, whenever he chooses to take it, but he no longer desires to be king. What, if anything, does he still want?

Something in Hamlet dies before the play opens, and I set aside the prevalent judgment that the deepest cause of his melancholia is his mourning for the dead father and his outrage at his mother's sexuality. Don't condescend to the Prince of Denmark: he is more intelligent than you are, whoever you are. That, ultimately, is why we need him and cannot evade his play. The foreground to Shakespeare's tragedy is Hamlet's consciousness of his own consciousness, unlimited yet at war with itself.

Though Shakespeare's overtly hermetist references are scattered elsewhere, sometimes in unlikely contexts, like *Coriolanus*, I belatedly agree with Dame Frances Yates that the Shakespearean Theater of the World has subtle links to visionaries like Giordano Bruno and Robert Fludd. Shakespeare was not like Victor Hugo and W. B. Yeats, an occultist, but then he was not any other single thing either, be it Catholic, royalist, or conservative. Preternaturally, he picked up anything useful to him that was available in his era. I hesitate to call any particular utterance by Hamlet a central statement, but this comes closest:

> *What piece of work is a man, how noble in reason, how infinite in faculties, in form and moving how express and admirable, in action how like an angel,* in apprehension how like a god . . . *[Emphasis mine]*
>
> [II.ii.303–307]

One knows that Shakespeare was not Pico della Mirandola—hermetist, Kabbalist, Neoplatonist—but Pico would have been happy to agree that in apprehension we could again be gods. Hamlet uniquely fuses apprehension and comprehension, and *could* be viewed as the hermetist Anthropos, or Man-God, come again. What could the professors at Lutheran Wittenberg have taught Hamlet, even in the arts of literature and theater? Hamlet potentially is a great poet-dramatist, like his creator, who attended no university. We do not (and need not) know Shakespeare's prime malaise, but we know Hamlet's: to be a mortal god in an immortal play. Any Fortinbras or Laertes could chop Claudius down; Hamlet knows he deserves the prime role in a cosmological drama, which Shakespeare was not quite ready to compose.

FIFTEEN

LET IT BE

The final act of *Hamlet* is a maelstrom, punctuated by its protagonist's admonitions: "Let be" and "let it be." Too wise not to sense the Claudius–Laertes plot, Hamlet nevertheless affirms his desire to come to an end of playacting:

> *I shall win at the odds. Thou wouldst not think how ill all's here about my heart; but it is no matter.*
>
> [V.ii.207–209]

A director might advise his Hamlet to slow down for "how ill all's here," since that wonderful "ill all's" needs to be sounded clearly. Horatio tries to hold off the end, but Hamlet will not:

> *Not a whit. We defy augury. There is special providence in the fall of a sparrow. If it be now, 'tis not to come. If it be not to come, it will be now. If it be not now, yet it will come. The readiness is all. Since no man of aught he leaves, knows aught, what is't to leave betimes? Let be.*

[V.ii.215–20]

I have repunctuated this intricate passage, according to my sense of it. Hamlet's New Testament references are personal, and have neither a Calvinist nor a Catholic aura. Clearly, he is audacious enough to adopt the accents of Jesus so as to appropriate them for the passion of his own betrayal (by Laertes) and his own sacrifice, though not to Yahweh alone, which was the stance of Jesus. If there is a precise providence in a sparrow's or a prince's fall, such providence nevertheless excludes Calvin's system. But what is "it"? "Death" can be only part of the answer: resolution of impasse is as large a part. Hamlet, weary of drama, casts his role definitively. "The readiness is all" may reflect the Geneva Bible's phrasing of Jesus' gentle irony concerning the disciple Peter asleep on watch: "The spirit indeed is ready, but the flesh is weak." Hamlet thrusts aside his natural fear of annihilation, in order to center upon what I judge to be a bitter rhetorical question: "What is't to leave betimes?" The precise moment of annihilation does not matter, because we know nothing about anything (or anyone) we leave behind. For Hamlet himself, death is not tragic, but an apotheosis.

SIXTEEN

APOTHEOSIS

AND TRAGEDY

*H*amlet, as a "poem unlimited," is too large for tragedy, though it is the tragedy of the Prince of Denmark. What is a tragedy, and what is an apotheosis?

Tragedy began as Dionysian song and dance, in archaic theater. Friedrich Nietzsche assimilated Hamlet to "the Dionysian man," and observed that Hamlet thought not too much, but much too well:

> *Not reflection, no—true knowledge, an insight into the*
> *horrible truth, outweighs any motive for action, both in*
> *Hamlet and in the Dionysian man.*

I once found this persuasive, but begin to doubt it, because I think that Hamlet was a new kind of man, and I have affirmed his affinities with the David of the Book of Samuel. The Dionysian is a very old kind of man: an ecstatic. Hamlet is as critical as he is creative, as rational as he is intuitive. He does not listen to the voice of the god, but rather to his own voice, which both mediates and expands his own consciousness of self. If Hamlet perishes of the truth, such truth is barely external. Hamlet *is* the truth, insofar as any hero of consciousness can be.

Every time I have managed to get through an entire performance of *Hamlet*—increasingly difficult these days—I have to admit that even my most intense rereadings of the play do not prepare me for the cognitive and aesthetic effect of Hamlet's death upon me. Apotheosis is an extraordinary challenge even to Shakespeare's powers of representation: how can you dramatize the exaltation of a human being to a seeming transcendence? Despite Horatio's loving evocation of flights of angels, Horatio and Hamlet seem to mean different things by "rest." Horatio may hint at resurrection, but Hamlet has experienced resurrection already, and may expect only the silence of annihilation. Shakespeare, who perhaps accepted that for nearly all his protagonists, wants something different for Hamlet. The prince may not be going to join Falstaff "in Arthur's bosom," yet he is going to move us to an apprehension of value gained rather than lost by his immolation. Though Hamlet's apotheosis is so difficult to describe, the audience's sense of it appears to be all but universal. Even to the most secular among us, Hamlet's death has vicarious resonances, though it cannot be called an atonement.

What Jesus still is to many believers, Hamlet still is to many skeptics: the exemplary figure. Shakespeare, whatever his personal convictions, did not compose either as believer or as skeptic. The passion of Hamlet (to call it that) seems more Davidic than Christlike, but then believers do accept David as Jesus' ancestor. Charisma gloriously expires upon stage, to our edification. We tend to feel augmented, rather than diminished, by Hamlet's death. The eloquence of the prince's departure, in the theater, has rivals in the last moments of Lear and of Macbeth, but possibly no rivals as a suggestion of apotheosis. How can Shakespeare attain so unique an effect when Hamlet overtly does not contend with supernal powers, but only with the wretched shuffler, Uncle Claudius?

The poet Swinburne, a good Shakespearean critic,

observed that "the signal characteristic of Hamlet's inner nature is by no means irresolution or hesitation or any form of weakness, but rather the strong conflux of contending forces." I think that is a clue to Hamlet's charisma, to his highly individual power over change and the final form of change—that is to say, over nature and death. Hamlet discovers that his life has been a quest with no object except his own endlessly burgeoning subjectivity. This truth, intolerable to any of us, helps turn Hamlet into an angel of destruction. Contending with unknown powers within his own self, the prince seems to struggle also with the spirit of evil in heavenly places.

Wrestling Jacob, hardly a foretype of Hamlet, held off a nameless one among the Elohim (perhaps the angel of death) and survived to win the new name of Israel. Hamlet, at the close, identifies himself with his own angel of death, and wins no new name. Indeed, he dreads bearing "a wounded name," and enjoins Horatio to go on to endlessly retell Hamlet the Dane's story. Breaking from his sources, Shakespeare gave the same name to the Hamlets, father and son, but they are as unlike as, say, Yahweh and Jesus, absurd as it is to compare the warrior-king to the God of Abraham, or the Son of Man to the prince of skeptics. And yet all comparison is rendered absurd by Hamlet's enigmatic apotheosis.

Both the play and his own sensibility confine Hamlet: he is too large for tragedy, for his own self, and weirdly too titanic for imaginative literature. Shakespeare, though he fought against his creature's transcendence of all forms, loses the battle in the final scenes. Paradoxically, what ought to have been (as T. S. Eliot argued) aesthetic failure became the most absolute of aesthetic triumph, by standards the character and the play pragmatically have invented. I have no idea whether Shakespeare intended Hamlet's apotheosis, but more than any other writer, he sets in motion energies that in themselves give the impression of being transcendental, rather than either personal or social. We do not know precisely how it is that we come to believe Hamlet has jeopardized his life in the high places of the field. Why are we persuaded that somehow Hamlet fights *for us*? That apparently infinite fascination of the figure stems from the enormous magnification of consciousness that it embodies, yet also from the refinement of consciousness into a quintessence that plausibly can intimate apotheosis.

SEVENTEEN

HAMLET AND
THE HIGH PLACES

W. H. Auden, ambivalent toward Hamlet, remarked that the prince's lack of faith both in God and in himself resulted in the stance of the player's or actor's constant state of performing. As I have admitted, the Hamlet of the first four acts seems to sustain just such a judgment, though I also have surmised that Shakespeare defended against Hamlet by thus rendering him histrionic. All of us in the audience share Shakespeare's ambivalence toward Hamlet, for on some level the prince frightens us as much as he attracts us. And yet the

Hamlet of the final scenes is very different. An aura of transcendence surrounds him, as here in the astonishing speech with which he seeks reconcilement with Laertes:

> *Give me your pardon, sir. I have done you wrong;*
> *But pardon't as you are a gentleman.*
> *This presence knows, and you must needs have heard,*
> *How I am punish'd with a sore distraction.*
> *What I have done*
> *That might your nature, honour, and exception*
> *Roughly awake, I here proclaim was madness.*
> *Was't Hamlet wrong'd Laertes? Never Hamlet.*
> *If Hamlet from himself be ta'en away,*
> *Then Hamlet does it not, Hamlet denies it.*
> *Who does it then? His madness. If't be so,*
> *Hamlet is of the faction that is wrong'd;*
> *His madness is poor Hamlet's enemy.*
> *Sir, in this audience,*
> *Let my disclaiming from a purpos'd evil*
> *Free me so far in your most generous thoughts*
> *That I have shot my arrow o'er the house*
> *And hurt my brother.*

> [V.ii.222–39]

Does Hamlet, then, believe in his former madness? Do we? When did it end? It began as an antic disposition, another weapon in the struggle with Claudius, and then was exploited by Hamlet, even abused until it bordered upon derangement. Each of us decides separately whether the border was crossed: I think not. And yet I do not find dissimulation in this noble speech. Hamlet is past that: he has moved from player to poet, but poetry, at its best, lies against time, and time's "It was" (to appropriate Nietzsche). Too prescient not to know that a plot is under way ("how ill all's here about my heart"), Hamlet is testing Laertes, and presumably does not believe the grudging response "I do receive your offer'd love like love / And will not wrong it." That is a mere lie, against the present, and I hear irony in Hamlet's rejoinder:

I embrace it freely,
And will this brother's wager frankly play—
[V.ii.252–53]

Hamlet the son, unlike Hamlet the father, is too knowing not to recognize another "brother's wager," akin to Claudius's murderous wager against the king. Wine cup and fencing foil are both poisoned, betraying how desperate Claudius has become. Hamlet discovers this almost as soon as we do, and goes into the duel spiritually prepared for it. Why, then, does he prelude Claudius's mousetrap with:

> . . . *I have shot my arrow o'er the house*
> *And hurt my brother.*
>
> [V.ii.243–44]

Laertes is too absurdly slight to be Hamlet's "second self," as many critics aver. He has very little of his sister Ophelia in him. Shakespeare lavishes everything upon Hamlet; there is little left for any other character in the play, the Grave-digger briefly excepted. Though Hamlet fences with great skill, is quick to return Laertes' poisoned thrust, and finishes off Claudius with brutal contempt, the prince's mind is disengaged, throughout this scene of slaughter. Conceding his own likely death when entering Claudius's trap, Hamlet is already in his own place, the high place of his dying. We can name that place only because it is Hamlet's, but no one else in the play, not even Horatio, will help us to recognize it. It is the place where even the most acute of all self-consciousnesses, Hamlet's, will lose the shadow of self while continuing to expand as a consciousness. What we have called Western Romanticism is the last embellishment of Hamlet's great shadow, cast off to become a thousand other selves.

EIGHTEEN

FORTINBRAS

The anti-Hamlet arrives with the belated reentrance of Fortinbras, who has marched over the stage, with his army, in Act IV, Scene iv. Hamlet enters there only after Fortinbras has exited, and the Norwegian prince parades into Elsinore a few lines after the Prince of Denmark's death. By this interesting ellipsis, Shakespeare emphasizes that Hamlet and Fortinbras never meet. Why are they kept apart?

Shakespearean omissions fascinate me: Lear and Edmund never exchange a word; Antony and Cleopatra, except for a moment, are not seen alone together; it is left uncertain whether Othello and Desdemona ever consummated their marriage. So sly is Shakespeare that Hamlet has time to mock the fop Osric but is not allowed to confront Fortinbras, whose father was slain by Hamlet's father, and who, like Hamlet, is blocked from the throne by an uncle.

Hamlet, with amiable irony, has termed Fortinbras "a delicate and tender prince" who marches off to Poland "to gain a little patch of ground" not large enough to bury those who will die disputing it. But Fortinbras is a head-basher, like his late father and like King Hamlet. It is another irony that Hamlet, who has just stabbed Claudius with the envenomed rapier, and then forced poisoned wine down his uncle's throat, prophesies that Fortinbras will be elected the new king of Denmark, and casts his own vote: "He has my dying voice."

Fortinbras has the final voice:

> *Let four captains*
> *Bear Hamlet like a soldier to the stage,*
> *For he was likely, had he been put on,*
> *To have prov'd most royal; and for his passage,*
> *The soldier's music and the rite of war*
> *Speak loudly for him.*

Take up the bodies. Such a sight as this
Becomes the field, but here shows much amiss.
Go, bid the soldiers shoot.

> [Exeunt marching, bearing off the bodies,
> after which a peal of ordnance is shot off.]

> [V.ii.400–409]

By "most royal," Fortinbras means "like father, like son," which is all he can understand. Shakespeare concludes the play with audacious irony: Hamlet receives full military honors, as if he too would have become a great killing machine. The largest representation we have of consciousness carried beyond conceivable limits is to be buried as though he were Henry V.

Fortinbras represents the world, but not the audience. Doubtless, Hamlet would have been courteous enough to Fortinbras had they met, but what could they have said to each other?

NINETEEN

HAD I BUT TIME—
O, I COULD TELL YOU

Our compact with Hamlet is that he will teach us who he is, and so instruct us in the mystery, the secret of his charismatic eminence. The mystery certainly is there. John Bayley shrewdly observed that if Hamlet beguiles us, we can assume he charmed Shakespeare also. We come to love what Shakespeare himself loved. Like Falstaff and Cleopatra, Hamlet bewilders me by his simultaneous excess in both theatricality and vitality. The *Henry IV* plays, *Antony and Cleopatra*, and *The Tragedy of Hamlet, Prince of Denmark* are unlimited poems, and yet seem confinements in proportion to

Falstaff, Cleopatra, and Hamlet. We want them to tell us even more than they do, because their power over language is so enormous.

Although critics have pointed out that Hamlet seems to meld Falstaff and Prince Hal in a single consciousness, it is also plausible to suggest that everything Shakespeare had composed before 1600 comes together in some aspect of the prince's nature. All the men and women imagined by the playwright are gathered up into a finer tone by Hamlet's voice. So profoundly does Hamlet study himself that we can be tempted to overlook how fiercely his ironical study is extended to others, not just all who throng his own play but also those who appear earlier in Shakespeare. It is Hamlet's triumph over Shakespeare (or perhaps Shakespeare's transcendence of Shakespeare) that the prince implicitly persuades us he knows more than his creator does.

There are two mysteries of Hamlet: one is theatrical, the other is visionary. The theatrical can be analyzed, though eventually the infinite experimentalism of the drama evades our instruments. But the visionary dimensions of what ought to be an actor's role trouble even the most rigorous and subtle of minds, like Hume's and

Wittgenstein's. Hamlet's *tone* is itself a vision. His voice testifies that what we see and feel comes from our narcissistic fall into what the hermetists called "love and sleep." Unloving and awake, Hamlet seems unfallen, not in a moral or theological sense, but as someone might be who, by glimpses, arrives beyond narcissism. By this, I mean the transmuted Hamlet of Act V, who fears a wounded name yet defies augury.

Earlier in the play, a more self-obsessed Hamlet tends to be most brilliantly ironic both in soliloquy and when taunting his gulls: Polonius and the ill-fated Guildenstern and Rosencrantz, wickedly undifferentiated by Shakespeare, thus creating literary space for Tom Stoppard. Since Hamlet kills Polonius (thinking him likely to be Claudius) and sends Rosencrantz and Guildenstern off to an English execution, their murders seem ungrateful of the prince, after they have provoked him to such cascades of dark wit:

> POLONIUS   —*What do you read, my lord?*
> HAMLET   *Words, words, words.*
> POLONIUS   *What is the matter, my lord?*
> HAMLET   *Between who?*

POLONIUS   *I mean the matter that you read, my lord.*

HAMLET   *Slanders, sir. For the satirical rogue says here that old men have gray beards, that their faces are wrinkled, their eyes purging thick amber and plum-tree gum, and that they have a plentiful lack of wit, together with most weak hams—all which, sir, though I most powerfully and potently believe, yet I hold it not honesty to have it thus set down. For yourself, sir, shall grow old as I am—if like a crab you could go backward.*

POLONIUS   [Aside] *Though this be madness, yet there is method in't.—Will you walk out of the air, my lord?*

HAMLET   *Into my grave?*

POLONIUS   *Indeed, that's out of the air.—[Aside] How pregnant sometimes his replies are—a happiness that often madness hits on, which reason and sanity could not so prosperously be delivered of. I will leave him and suddenly contrive the means of meeting between him and my daughter.—My lord, I will take my leave of you.*

HAMLET   *You cannot, sir, take from me anything that I will not more willingly part withal—except my life, except my life, except my life.*

[II.ii.191–217]

That thrice-uttered "except my life" conveys authentic desperation, which will be raised to the sublime by friction with the false college chums, Rosenstern and Guildencrantz (for the sake of variety):

Why, look you now, how unworthy a thing you make of me. You would play upon me, you would seem to know my stops, you would pluck out the heart of my mystery, you would sound me from my lowest note to the top of my compass; and there is much music, excellent voice, in this little organ, yet cannot you make it speak. 'Sblood, do you think I am easier to be played on than a pipe? Call me what instrument you will, though you fret me, you cannot play upon me.

[III.ii.354–63]

We cannot play upon him, and we begin to wonder if Shakespeare always can make him speak. Hamlet throughout, but particularly after his return from the sea, knows something we want and need to know, and part of his play's power over us is that we ransack it hoping to find out the secret. We are "guilty creatures sitting at a play," wondering if its cunning will prompt us to proclaim our malefactions. Each time I read, teach, or attend *Hamlet*, I am struck hardest by the prince's dying intimation of what has been undivulged:

> *You that look pale and tremble at this chance,*
> *That are but mutes or audience to this act,*
> *Had I but time—as this fell sergeant, Death,*
> *Is strict in his arrest—O, I could tell you—*
> *But let it be.*

[V.ii.339–43]

Hamlet utters a total of almost twenty more lines after that "let it be," so that one can experience a certain frustration at not being told part, at least, of what is hinted. We are addressed specifically *as audience*, reminding us again of how readily this play has forsaken its supposed function of representation and instead has offered itself to us as the thing itself. Hamlet, by presenting himself as an authorial consciousness—by no means Shakespeare's own—is no longer a part for a player. He is one of us, and yet possesses the knowledge of how we relate to him.

He wants us, the unsatisfied, to exonerate him, lest he bear a wounded name. That wager he goes on winning:

you have to be quite an advanced literary critic *not* to love him, hardly an original observation for me to make. Yet he seems to want to tell us something beyond our relationship to him. He says that he is already dead, an acknowledgment he could have made in the graveyard. Unlike his father, he is not a ghost, but a resurrected spirit about to die, in the pattern of the Jesus of the Gnostic heretics. I suggest that had he time, he could tell us something about "the undiscover'd country, from whose bourn / No traveller returns."

TWENTY

ANNIHILATION: HAMLET'S WAKE

Though Horatio expects Hamlet to be carried directly off to heaven, that prospect seems irrelevant, as does the Ghost's hellish account of his purgatory. Hamlet the son is not going to heaven, hell, purgatory, or limbo, or to any other theological fantasy. He has been there, done that, in his exhaustive drama. The hero of the poem unlimited cannot be envisioned embarking on a final voyage to the imagined lands of the Catholics, Calvinists, or Lutherans. He knows what he taught Emerson: "As men's prayers are a disease of the Will, so are their creeds a disease of the Intellect."

Hamlet, a bookish swordsman, clearly has read Montaigne, Emerson's forerunner. Perhaps he is carrying the *Essays* about with him when Polonius accosts him. Montaigne advised us not to bother to prepare for dying, because we would know well enough how to do it when the time came. Pragmatically, that is Hamlet's stance. Silence is the salient aspect of what is coming for all of us, and Hamlet has been anything but a silent protagonist. What can the world do with a silent Hamlet?

For Hamlet, silence is annihilation. Hamlet's wake, his name, has not been wounded but wondrous: Ibsen and Chekhov, Pirandello and Beckett have rewritten him, and so have the novelists Goethe, Scott, Dickens, Melville, and Joyce. Playwrights and novelists will be compelled to continue revising Hamlet, for reasons that I suspect have more to do with our horror of our own consciousness confronting annihilation than with our individual addictions to guilt and to grief.

What matters most about Hamlet is his genius, which is for consciousness itself. He is aware that his inner self perpetually augments, and that he must go on overhearing an ever-burgeoning self-consciousness. Only annihilation is the alternative to self-overhearing, for nothing else can stop Hamlet's astonishing gift of awareness.

I want to be as clear as I can be about Hamlet's stance: it is pragmatically nihilist, which does not rule out spiritual yearnings, whether Catholic, Protestant, or hermetist (in the manner of Giordano Bruno, as Frances Yates suggested). Hamlet is a god in ruins, which was Emerson's Orphic definition of man. To know that you are a fallen divinity is a difference that makes a difference: annihilation becomes a welcome alternative.

Any exegesis of *Hamlet* takes place within the circle of the play's endless notoriety: this remains the literary work proper, the thing itself, what first we think of when we consider the experience of the reader, or of the auditor. We all are celebrants at Hamlet's wake: Russians, Germans, Celts, wandering Jews, Asians, Africans. Universality is Hamlet's glory, or is it now his stigma? In relation to the prince, we are rather like Hamlet himself in regard to the Grave-digger:

How absolute the knave is. We must speak by the card or equivocation will undo us.

[V.i.137–38]

We need the shipman's card, on which all thirty-two compass points clearly are marked, but no such chart is available to us. Where everything is questionable, we have not just several plays in one, but ultimately a player too equivocal for any of his plays.

King Lear has a stop, as does *Macbeth*; *Hamlet* does not. We exit believing that Lear has told us everything he had to tell, and that Macbeth has exhausted tale-telling. Hamlet, as seen, tantalizes us with what he has not the time to divulge. If drama takes dictionary definition, it tells a story for performance, one that begins and ends. There is an end to *Hamlet,* but not to Hamlet: he comes alive at the wake. His whoreson dead body, after four centuries, has not decayed.

The Grave-digger, Hamlet's only worthy interlocutor, blocks the prince's wit with superb gamesmanship:

'Tis a quick lie, sir, 'twill away again from me to you.
[V.i.128]

The question at issue is: Whose grave is it? Rhetorically, the undertaker wins in this duet, but in truth we do not believe him, for where shall he bury Hamlet? In dy-

ing, Goethe's imitation Hamlet, Faust, declares his satis-
faction, and so is satisfactorily buried, unlike Goethe,
who speculated that some exemption from dying might
be arranged, in the scheme of things, for a consciousness
as creative as his own.

TWENTY-ONE

THE FUSION OF HIGH
AND POPULAR ART

A "poem unlimited" should be the greatest of enter-
tainments, but I have yet to see *Hamlet* performed,
on screen or stage, as extravagantly as it should be done.
I hasten to stammer, "No! I don't mean *Hamlet* the
musical!" What is wanted is a director and an actor who
are monsters of consciousness, and who can keep up
with that true combat of mighty opposites, Hamlet and
Shakespeare. In such a death duel, I would want the actor to side with Shakespeare, and the director to favor
Hamlet. Let the actor underplay, even as he is over-
directed.

As audience, we thus will confront a protagonist and a director in dubious battle, but that should help emphasize that everything in the play that is not Hamlet himself is peculiarly archaic. The actor will imply continuously that he has been dropped into the wrong play, yet feels it will do as badly, or as well, as any other, while the director will maintain pressure to evidence that Hamlet is far too good for this antique vehicle, which could wheeze along with just a commonplace hero (or hero-villain) at the center.

Scholarship has not been able to establish the precise relationship of *Hamlet* to its key-source, an earlier *Hamlet* generally ascribed to Thomas Kyd, author of *The Spanish Tragedy,* a great audience pleaser in Shakespeare's day but dear now only to specialists. I continue to follow Peter Alexander in his surmise that the first *Hamlet* was composed by the very young Shakespeare himself. Hidden inside the final *Hamlet* is the ghost of the first one, including the archaic Ghost, ironically played by Shakespeare, perhaps as one more in-joke.

Who, besides Hamlet (and the Grave-digger), can sustain prolonged analysis of the final play? The entire cast are mindless shadows when confronted by the bookish, theatergoing, skeptical prince, who seems centuries later than everyone else, including the audience. We have not caught up to the Hamlet of Act V, because he thinks more comprehensively than most of us can. That Hamlet of earlier acts can be more problematical: can he truly be the maniac moralizer he plays at being in the closet scene, where his sadistic rhetoric is so disconcerting?

I don't know that anything else in literature gives us so amazing a fusion of high and popular art as the confrontation between Hamlet and Gertrude in Act III, Scene iv, which goes on for more than two hundred lines, much of it given over to high Hamletian rant:

Let the bloat King tempt you again to bed,
Pinch wanton on your cheek, call you his mouse,
And let him, for a pair of reechy kisses,
Or paddling in your neck with his damn'd fingers,
Make you to ravel all this matter out
That I essentially am not in madness,
But mad in craft. 'Twere good you let him know,
For who that's but a queen, fair, sober, wise,
Would from a paddock, from a bat, a gib,
Such dear concernings hide? Who would do so?

No, in despite of sense and secrecy,
Unpeg the basket on the house's top,
Let the birds fly, and like the famous ape,
To try conclusions, in the basket creep,
And break your own neck down.

[III.iv.184–98]

Mad in craft indeed, and very dangerous, this Hamlet is at once pre-Shakespearean and postmodern, and certainly at home in the rhetoric of proverb and fable. Rather nastily, the prince informs his mother that telling Claudius of an assumed madness will bring her end also in the general catastrophe, a perfectly accurate prophecy. Such a tirade is addressed both to the groundlings and to the nobility, to delight the former by familiarity and the latter by an easy descent to the communal. Throughout the closet scene, Hamlet mixes high and low rhetoric with the antic glee of a player cutting loose from his playwright, boisterously breaking all the rules of representation:

O shame, where is thy blush?
Rebellious hell,
If thou canst mutine in a matron's bones,

To flowing youth let virtue be as wax
And melt in her own fire.

[III.iv.81–85]

Reflection makes us murmur that it does not need a Hamlet to mouth this fustian stuff, but the staged scene allows no pause for such realization. We go from the manslaughter of the wretched Polonius through the singular reentry of the Ghost and on to Hamlet's grim prediction that he will explode Rosencrantz and Guildenstern at the moon. By the time the prince exits, dragging Polonius's corpse with him, we are still startled by his casual brutality: "I'll lug the guts into the neighbour room." Melodramatic farce is domesticated in this freest and wildest of plays, where anything may happen, and expectation is invoked largely to be confounded.

TWENTY–TWO

HAMLET
AS THE LIMIT
OF STAGE DRAMA

S hakespeare's only son, Hamnet, died at age eleven
in 1596. John Shakespeare, the poet's father, died in
1601. At thirty-seven, Shakespeare had lost both. Whatever relation this had to *Hamlet* has to be conjectural,
and was most eloquently propounded by James Joyce's
Stephen Dedalus in the Library scene of *Ulysses*:

> —*Sabellius, the African, subtlest heresiarch of all
> the beasts of the field, held that the Father was Himself
> His Own Son. The bulldog of Aquin, with whom no*

word shall be impossible, refutes him. Well: if the fa-
ther who has not a son be not a father can the son who has
not a father be a son? When Rutlandbaconsouthampton-
shakespeare or another poet of the same name in the
comedy of errors wrote Hamlet *he was not the father of*
his own son merely but, being no more a son, he was and
felt himself the father of all his race, the father of his
own grandfather, the father of his unborn grandson
who, by the same token, never was born. . . .

If *Hamlet* constitutes, to whatever degree, a meditation upon fathers and sons—and most of us agree with
that notion—the context for dramatic brooding on filial
matters is observed by the overt enigmas of stage representation. The black prince, a dramatic individual, comes
to understand that he has been mourning the idea of
fatherhood/sonship rather than the actual King Hamlet,
an uxorious killing machine with whom the great solil-
oquist has absolutely nothing in common. When the
Ghost, who seems to have undergone rather minimal
character change in Purgatory, glides onto the closet
scene, he still demands Claudius's blood. As in Act I, he
is unconcerned with his son's well-being, but instead
becomes alarmed at Gertrude's psychic condition. The

prince, in the Ghost's view, is to be a sword of vengeance: no more nor less.

Shakespeare, despite much scholarly argument to the contrary, was no lover of authority, which had murdered Christopher Marlowe, tortured and broken Thomas Kyd, and branded Ben Jonson. The poet kept some distance from the ruling powers, and temporized whenever necessary. Are we to believe that Hamlet loves authority? He *tries*, but it will not work. Even the Ghost, supposed image of the play's only authentic authority, is soon enough addressed by his son as "truepenny" and "old mole," and referred to as "this fellow in the cellarage." Hamlet's mourning, of which we continue to make too much, has equivocal elements. Like Samuel Beckett, who wrote his own *Hamlet* in *Endgame*, the prince is sorrier for humankind than he is for himself.

You cannot reduce Hamlet to any consistency, even in his grief. His drama is limitless precisely because his personality is informed by his own cognitive power, which appears unbounded. Since, in Hamlet's case, the play *is* the figure, we pragmatically cannot hold this, of all Shakespeare's dramas, together in our minds. Samuel Johnson, properly puzzled and not enthralled, said, "We must allow to the tragedy of *Hamlet* the praise of variety." One agrees with Johnson's mordant observation: "The apparition left the regions of the dead to little purpose," for the plot cannot change Hamlet. Only Hamlet can, by hearing his own formulations, and then thinking himself beyond them. Not just the most experimental of plays, *Hamlet* truly is the graveyard of drama. Shakespeare escaped from *Hamlet* to write *Othello* and *King Lear, Macbeth* and *Antony and Cleopatra,* but no one else—playwright or novelist—quite gets out of that burial ground. Our deep subjectivity hovers there, its emblem the skull of Yorick.

Iago was the solution that Shakespeare's genius found to the impasse Hamlet constitutes. The prince would not deign to say, "For I am nothing if not critical." Iago constructs his own isolation; Hamlet already is isolation. Shakespeare uses Iago to get started again, but with no ambition to go beyond Hamlet, which may be impossible. Even where the prince has only the absurd (Osric) to comment upon, his commentary nevertheless transcends its own prophecy:

A did comply with his dug before a sucked it. Thus has he—and many more of the same bevy that I know the drossy age dotes on—only got the tune of the time and,

out of an habit of encounter, a kind of yeasty collection,
which carries them through and through the most fanned
and winnowed opinions; and do not but blow them to
their trial, the bubbles are out.

[V.ii.184–91]

Osric here stands in not only for a flock of contemporary courtiers, but for fashionable rival playwrights, and possibly for most of us as well, whoever we are. It is the dramatic placement of the Osric follies that startles: Hamlet is aware he is about to enter Claudius's last entrapment, in the duel with Laertes. To call his stance "insouciant" would undervalue it. As always, he mocks the play: plot, ethos, context.

Shakespeare partly answers Hamlet's irony by an enormous advance in the representations of villains: Iago, Edmund in *King Lear,* Macbeth. Extraordinary as these are, they do not bruise the demarcations between their plays and reality. Hamlet's undiscovered country, his embassy of annihilation, voids the limits that ought to confine his drama to stage dimensions.

Ransacking *Hamlet* is a losing process. If, as with an open box, you could turn the entire play over and empty it out, its scattered contents would defy reassembly into the spunkily coherent entity that goes on sublimely transcending the sum of its components. The malaise that haunts Elsinore is not the unrevenged regicide, or the other corruptions of the shuffling Claudius, but the negative power of Hamlet's consciousness. Of all Shakespeare's subtle ellipses, Hamlet is the crown. No two directors, critics, actors, readers, auditors ever can agree on the center of Hamlet's being. Victor Hugo, always infectiously outrageous, saw Hamlet as a new Prometheus, presumably thefting the fire of divine consciousness in order to augment the genius of humankind. Scholars scoff at Hugo; I revere him. Though one wonders, How can you be a Prometheus in a cosmos devoid of a Zeus? Unsponsored and free, Hamlet longs for a mighty opposite, and discovers he has to be his own. He inaugurates the situation in which each of us has to be our own worst enemy.

Is that the stuff to be quarried by dramatic art? *Hamlet*, Goethe remarked, already is a novel, but so is what scholars call the Henriad: *Richard II*, the two parts of *Henry IV*, and *Henry V*. Falstaff, like Hamlet, is a cosmos too vast for stage representation, as Lear may be also. But *Hamlet* the play, while it has fostered many novels, ruggedly seems something other than novelistic, though that something has little to do with revenge tragedy. Hamlet's self-enmity is not Dostoevskian or Conradian-Faulknerian. Despite his musings, he is the least likely of suicides, unlike his imitators Svidrigailov, Decoud in *Nostromo*, and Quentin Compson.

Like several critics before me, I have located the dramaturgical crisis of *Hamlet* in the closet scene—which, however, I do not interpret either as family romance or as another play-within-the-play. Hamlet, so individual everywhere else, is absolutely bizarre in his language as he confronts his mother (as has been seen), tub-thumping away like an American televangelist denouncing sin. Shakespeare threw away all decorum of diction by inventing Hamlet, who will not ever shut up or confine himself to courtly conventions.

Since *Hamlet* is perpetually revived on stages everywhere, palpably it works as a play, though by all rational standards it should not. Every production that I've seen thins the complexities out, wishing them away. We set limits upon the poem unlimited, thus warding off what it is in Hamlet himself we cannot assimilate, an apprehension of mortality a touch too sharp to bear:

O that that earth which kept the world in awe
Should patch a wall t'expel the winter's flaw.

[V.i.213–14]

Hamlet, in the graveyard, jests on "Imperious Cae-sar," but all of us are Adamic, earth to earth. Common-place as a reminder, this would be intolerable if we had to maintain it in consciousness constantly, for all our re-maining moments. Staged with fitting force, *Hamlet* would be drama transfigured to a death march.

TWENTY-THREE

THE END
OF OUR TIME

As an archetype of the artist, Hamlet has been iden-
tified with a range of incarnations from Jesus
Christ through William Shakespeare on to Oscar Wilde.
Amiably outrageous, these identifications (and others)
will continue: much of literature since the later eighteenth
century emanates from strong misreadings of *Hamlet*.
It is difficult to conceive of Goethe, Chekhov, or Joyce
without *Hamlet*. Dostoevsky, Ibsen, and Proust turned
elsewhere in Shakespeare, in search of a nihilism less
ambivalent than Hamlet's, since a residual idealism in
the prince tempers the bleakness of his quest for annihi-

lation. Pirandello, who continually rewrote *Hamlet*, may be the central modern playwright, as Eric Bentley argues, yet Beckett still seems the end of our time, even in these opening years of the twenty-first century. *Endgame* has much more to do with *Hamlet* than with *King Lear*, and probably qualifies as the most creative misreading of Shakespeare's notorious play in the later twentieth century.

Theatricality is as natural to Beckett's protagonists as it is to Hamlet, and as it seems not to have been to Beckett himself. Sometimes I am tempted to believe that Shakespeare as a person resembled Chekhov and Beckett, both of them humane and wise individuals, free of authorial egomania. The Borgesian vision of Shakespeare as everyone and no one seems also applicable to Chekhov and to Beckett. It is not relevant to any of Shakespeare's greatest characters: Falstaff and Hamlet, Iago and Cleopatra, Lear and the Fool. Hamlet is the antithesis of Everyman: in the contrast between ordinary citizen and alienated artist-intellectual, he always provides the model for the latter, as he did for Joyce's Stephen Dedalus. Leopold Bloom, extraordinary citizen, may have been Joyce's vision both of Joyce and of Shakespeare. Curious, kindly, perceptive, shrewd, and gentle, Poldy is the anti-Hamlet to Stephen's self-obsessed prince.

The end of Hamlet, in the twentieth century, came as the surly Hamm of *Endgame:* solipsistic, white-eyed, and a blind, monstrous temperament, but a capacious consciousness, steeped in balked creativity, and above all an overt actor, engrossed by his own theatricality. *Endgame* is a play within a play, enclosed by *Hamlet.* Like the prince's, Hamm's is an authorial consciousness run wild and turned destructive. Hamm is a poet, but in the dreadful sense in which the murderous Mao was a poet. They rely on the power of their texts to claw, which was Beckett's remark on *Endgame.*

SINCE *HAMLET,* and not its child, *Endgame,* is this little book's subject, I want to see if Beckett's implicit interpretation of *Hamlet* (his creative misreading) can illuminate the millennial aspect of Shakespeare's play, which was composed at the turn into the seventeenth century. In *Hamlet's* first scene, Horatio preludes the Ghost's second entrance by speaking of eclipses in the sun and moon, which had taken place in 1598, prompting apocalyptic forebodings concerning 1600:

As stars with trains of fire and dews of blood,
Disasters in the sun; and the moist star,
Upon whose influence Neptune's empire stands,
Was sick almost to doomsday with eclipse.
And even the like precurse of fear'd events,
As harbingers preceding still the fates
And prologue to the omen coming on,
Have heaven and earth together demonstrated
Unto our climatures and countrymen.

[I.i.120–28]

Gloucester in *King Lear* thinks back uneasily to these late eclipses, but Edmund zestfully mocks them. There is an apocalyptic edge to *King Lear*. We are less accustomed to thinking of *Hamlet* as an end-piece, yet its ambivalences, to me, portend a more profound nihilism than is embodied in *King Lear* and in *Macbeth*. Hamlet does not say that the state is out of joint, but the time; and his acceptance of Claudius's final entrapment is the defiant "what is't to leave betimes? Let be."

OUR PASSAGE into a kind of end-time was marked by presages in 2001, well before the catastrophe of

September 11. Historians, though, are likely to see the destruction of the World Trade Center as the overt beginning of what could turn out to be a hundred years' war between extremist Islamism and the West. There are no overt wars of religion in *Hamlet*, only land grabbings, while a general sentiment of the problematics of royal succession hovers throughout the play, exemplified in the contrasting crown princes, Hamlet and Fortinbras. Elizabeth was to die in 1603, to be followed by James I, son of Mary, Queen of Scots. Shakespeare in *Hamlet* seems to shunt aside contemporary political decline, even as the Earl of Essex waned toward his disastrous coup and subsequent beheading in 1601.

Scholars surmise that the malaise of Claudius's court is a distant reflection of the anxieties gathering in a London unsure of the post-Elizabethan future. Perhaps there is an undersong in *Hamlet*: Shakespeare already has seen the best of his time. All this seems secondary to the play's prolonged meditation upon death, with the acceptance, pragmatic and nihilistic, of annihilation.

Hamlet in Act V passes into a stance that is indescribable: call it quietism, disinterestedness, wise passivity, or what one will. Frank Kermode suggests that "Hamlet's part is compliance" with a universal plan, a providence "inexplicable and painful." That is to honor one of Hamlet's own formulations, which seems to me too equivocal to be trusted. There always is something else in Hamlet, an excessiveness that uncreates the providential. It is in the spirit of that excess that Hamlet foresees the end of his time, surrendering himself to process, to a flow of events that Claudius cannot stage-manage. Much more even than in *Endgame,* we conclude as at a theater, but staring out at the audience, as the actors do. Hamlet's part includes compliance, but with what plan is uncertain.

TWENTY-FOUR

THE HERO OF
CONSCIOUSNESS

The history of the inward self has been written by many scholars and psychologists working from an extraordinary variety of perspectives. The Dutch psychologist J. H. van den Berg, in his *The Changing Nature of Man*, traced the birth of self-inwardness to Luther's essay on Christian freedom (1520). Protestantism is certainly relevant to the augmentation of self-consciousness, which became both a supreme value and a terrible burden in Romanticism. I suspect, though, that Hamlet, more than Luther, was the prime origin of Romantic self-consciousness.

Can even Hamlet, the genius of Western consciousness, find his way back from his knowledge of the void
to a second and higher innocence? I do not find what
Blake called "Organized Innocence" even in the Hamlet
of Act V. Only Hamlet's mind can defend against its
own terrible force, and the unrelenting theatricalist in
him refuses to cease indulging in dramatic irony. He will
not allow himself to forget that he is another staged
representation, even as we refuse to bear that always
in mind.

Unlike Oedipus or Lear, Hamlet never seems victim-
ized by dramatic irony. What perspectives can we turn
upon Hamlet other than those he himself has revealed
to us? Hamlet's power of mind exceeds ours: we haven't
the authority to regard him ironically. For all his brilliance, Oedipus the King—and not the blind wanderer
at Colonus—is contrived by Sophocles to know less than
the audience does. Hamlet's unique relation to the audience is just the reverse: he knows that he knows more.

Thomas Carlyle, who esteemed Shakespeare above
all other *thinkers*, praised what he called the poet's "unconscious intellect," meaning by "unconsciousness" that
"the healthy know not of their health, but only the sick."
Carlyle, absurdly unread these days, may have erred,

very subtly. Health and sickness are not contrasts in
Hamlet: he is sick, after all, only north-by-northwest,
and I do not believe in his madness, the antic disposi-
tion of a great ironist. Perhaps Falstaff, Cleopatra, and
Lear emerge from Shakespeare's "unconscious intellect";
Hamlet and Iago do not.

If you think your way through to the truth, then you
must die of it: that Nietzschean interpretation of Hamlet,
which once pleased me, now also seems subtly wrong. It
is dangerous to affirm that Hamlet himself is the truth;
Christian believers would regard that as blasphemy. Yet
I do not know what else to call Hamlet; there is a God
within him, and he speaks: "And yet, to me, what is this
quintessence of dust?" Hamlet's is the most refined of
all Adamic dusts, but remains the Old Adam and not the
New: essentially dust.

WE GO back to Hamlet because we cannot achieve
enough consciousness, even at the expense of a sicken-
ing self-consciousness. In the Hebrew Bible, David is
a new kind of man, as is his descendant, Jesus, in the
Greek New Testament. Hamlet marks a third newness,
secularized and destructive. Shakespeare, playing with

the limits of stage representation, shows an ironic awareness of the unprecedentedness of his creation. The Hamlets, father and son, must share the same name, though they possess nothing else in common. Are we certain we know everything the prince means in his early exchange with Horatio?

HAMLET   *My father—methinks I see my father—*
HORATIO   *Where, my lord?*
HAMLET   *In my mind's eye, Horatio.*
HORATIO   *I saw him once; a was a goodly king.*
HAMLET   *A was a man, take him for all in all:*
   I shall not look upon his like again.

[I.ii.184–88]

There is more awe than love in that judgment, and a great wisdom in "take him for all in all." Hamlet's explorations in consciousness turn upon the question "What is man?" which in him is not an Oedipal concern. Perhaps it is the invention of ambivalence, as we have come to know it. Hamlet sees himself as nothing and everything, like his creator Shakespeare, famously regarded by Jorge Luis Borges as no one and everyone. We read or attend *Hamlet* and bring our own ambivalences with us, but the prince alters and deepens them. When he dies, our modified ambivalences, now set upon him, ring the hero in an aura that is a kind of taboo. Hamlet has bruised the limits for all of us in carrying out his embassy of death. If we remain in a harsh world where, with Horatio, we will draw our breath in pain, it is because we are not yet ready to accept Hamlet's judgment that the obliteration of consciousness is an absolute felicity. He departs before us, unforgettable as disturbance and as icon.

TWENTY-FIVE

HAMLET
AND NO END

Goethe, though secure on his German Olympus, never got over Shakespeare, or *Hamlet*. At sixty-six he wrote the essay "Schäkespear und Kein Ende!" or "No End of Shakespeare!" This ambivalent performance was prompted by Goethe's botching of *Romeo and Juliet* in his own translated travesty, which is hideously inadequate to the vibrant original. With *Hamlet,* no fresh botching was necessary; Goethe had been rewriting it all his life, and was still at it in the Second Part of *Faust*.

King Hamlet's end is reached quickly enough: we don't like the Ghost, and we would have liked the warrior-king still less. Yet none of us can discover the limits of Hamlet's consciousness, nor can we compel Shakespeare's "poem unlimited" to stay inert long enough so that we can contemplate it fully as an aesthetic artifact. As this is the last of my twenty-five brief chapters, I intend to devote it to surmise. What was it in Shakespeare, as poet-dramatist and as person, that broke loose in *Hamlet* and in Hamlet? What was he trying to do for himself, as creator and as creature?

Hamlet intervenes chronologically between *As You Like It* and *Twelfth Night,* high comedies with which it shares more than it does with *Othello, King Lear,* or *Macbeth.* Hamlet himself is a master comedian, like Falstaff, Rosalind, and Feste. The play's most famous image is the prince contemplating the skull of Yorick, the royal jester. If it is anyone's play besides Hamlet's and the Grave-digger's, it is Yorick's, whose Ghost should have returned in place of King Hamlet's.

Yorick has been dead for twenty-three years, and is still unforgiven by the Grave-digger, as a "whoreson mad fellow," a royal who poured a flagon of wine on the Grave-digger's reverend head. Hamlet's spiritual father, Yorick would have been of more use to his onetime playfellow than is Horatio, straightest of straight men.

But Yorick is dead, doubtless gone to Arthur's Bosom with Falstaff, and Hamlet reigns alone as monarch of wit in a witless kingdom.

Hamlet's isolation, as I interpret it, is Shakespeare's own. There is a tradition, which we ought to honor, that Shakespeare went to his deathbed after a night of serious drinking with Ben Jonson and Michael Drayton, who had come up from London to Stratford to cheer their old friend. They went back the next day; he died.

Who was Shakespeare's closest friend? Certainly not the great bear Jonson, whom he had bested in the wars of wit, and probably not the genial Drayton, but in truth we just do not know. Shakespeare seems to have been a gregarious loner, the most preternatural of observers and of gleaners. Like his Hamlet, he was a questioner. Harry Levin usefully observed that the word "question" is used seventeen times in Hamlet, far more often than in any of the other plays. What does Hamlet not question, in this tragic farce?

Something, doubtless Claudius, is rotten in Denmark, and yet *Hamlet* has nothing of the rancidity of *Troilus and Cressida* and *Measure for Measure*. Though he is both dangerous and conniving, something in Hamlet remains normative, almost wholesome. Of Shakespeare's affection, however disinterested, for this protagonist-of-protagonists, we need not doubt, though everything else in the play is doubtful. How can it contain Hamlet, who tolerates no confinements?

Of Hamlet's peers in Shakespeare, Falstaff and Rosalind precede him, while Iago and Cleopatra come later. The passion of Lear belongs to another order of representation, as does Macbeth's trafficking with the night world. Most scholars wince or guffaw when I assert the normativeness of Falstaff: highwayman, eating-and-drinking machine, perhaps confidence man above all. But wit is normative in and to Shakespeare, and Falstaff is wittier even than Rosalind and Hamlet, and slyer beyond Iago and Cleopatra, and Shakespeare is benignly, endlessly sly.

Rosalind is the normative center in Shakespeare: good will, charm, the innocence of language at its most intelligent, benignity that refuses power over other selves. Hamlet, in a history or a comedy, would have delighted in Falstaff and Rosalind. But he has been placed in a poem unlimited masking as revenge tragedy, where his isolation is absolute. Something in Shakespeare seeks isolation for his most gifted protagonist, so as to test his

own limits at dramatic representation. The poet found
he had no such limits.

What did Shakespeare the person find? Not a confrontation with the tragic muse, since he went on first to
Twelfth Night, and entered tragedy again only after the
death of comedy in the dark triad of *Troilus and Cressida, All's Well That Ends Well,* and *Measure for Measure.* I think he found himself and recoiled from the
finding. There is no end to *Hamlet* or to Hamlet, because
there is no end to Shakespeare.

He had discovered the nature of the selfsame, the full
secret of how to represent an identity. Perhaps he has
vindicated his own powers, if (as I believe) the much
earlier *Hamlet* of the late 1580s was his also, but he was
not much concerned with vindication. It is true that the
dying Hamlet fears he will survive as a wounded name,
and some of the Sonnets feature Shakespeare's own anxiety at something like that. But the Sonnet sequence is
hardly a monument of anxiety, and it designedly blocks
any clear entry to Shakespeare's own inwardness.

Falstaff, in his novelistic inwardness, is one way into
Shakespeare's center; Hamlet is another. Shakespeare
will not let Falstaff die upon stage. The greatest of comic

geniuses dies in Mistress Quickly's account in *Henry V.*
Hamlet dies an extraordinarily extended death: it takes
nearly sixty lines from the fatal wound through "the rest
is silence." There is no reason it could not go on for
six hundred lines: Hamlet would continue to dazzle us.
His play of some four thousand lines is Shakespeare's
longest and yet it is not long enough. We want to hear
Hamlet on everything, as we hear Montaigne, Goethe,
Emerson, Nietzsche, Freud. Shakespeare, having broken into the mode of the poem unlimited, closed it so
that always we would go on needing to hear more.